# 37 MORE VOICES

# BY APPLE AN

## Fiction

*Mother of Red Mountains*
*Daughter of Blue City*

## Memoir

*Las Crosses*

## Nonfiction Anthology

*28 Voices*
*37 More Voices*

## Nonfiction Self-Help

*All-in-One Dotted Journal Notebook*

# By Georgia A. Popoff

**Poetry**

*Living with Haints*

*Psychometry*

*Psalter: The Agnostic's Book of Common Curiosities*

*The Doom Weaver*

*Coaxing Nectar from Longing*

**Nonfiction**

*The Whiskey of Our Discontent: Gwendolyn Brooks as Conscience &*
*Change Agent*

*Our Difficult Sunlight: A Guide to Poetry, Literacy, & Social Justice*
*in Classroom & Community*

**Anthology**

*28 Voices*

*37 More Voices*

*Voices in Verse*

# 37 More Voices

## Voices Heard Anthology Series
## Vol. 2

Edited and
with an Introduction by
**Apple An & Georgia A. Popoff**

Foreword by
**Gwenlyn Davis**

Voices Heard Publishing, LLC

Cover background photo by Kevin Morrow

Cover design by Susan Keeter

Artwork rendering by Apple An

Library of Congress Control Number 2025917548

ISBN: 978-1-958900-23-9 (hardcover)

978-1-958900-22-2 (paperback)

978-1-958900-21-5 (ebook)

1st Edition, 1st Printing: October 2025

2nd Printing: November 2025

# DEDICATION

*To my writing instructors, fellow writers, and many inspiring authors.*
– Apple An

*To all the writers of the Writers Voice community, and especially the Flowbies and DWC PRO students over the years.*
– Georgia A. Popoff

# Acknowledgements

For 25 years, the YMCA of Central NY's Writers Voice / Downtown Writers Center (DWC) has provided a community in which writers in all phases of their development have and continue to learn, with and from each other. We thank the Writers Voice for supporting the work of those who appear on these pages.

We are grateful to the volunteers who have donated their talent, time, and effort to the collection. Thanks to Susan Keeter for her artistic talent and keen eye on the cover design, and to Kevin Morrow for his beautiful photo gracing this second volume. We appreciate Gwenlyn Davis for her heartfelt and thoughtful foreword.

And to the contributors, the editors appreciate your stories and how you have told them. It is a privilege to present them to the world.

# Contents

# FOREWORD

## Gwenlyn Davis

The Downtown Writers Center (DWC) at the YMCA in Syracuse, NY, is that spot on a map where I began attending in-person writing classes in 2015. Writer's Voice is a newer name for the Y's writing programs, which includes the DWC. That's the launchpad where my writing was born and raised alongside other aspiring scribes wanting to tell their stories. We sat shoulder-to-shoulder around ample tables in snug classrooms lined with shelves of books. Since the pandemic, with Zoom, most classes are now offered with worldwide elbow room.

Those first steps I took through the doors of the DWC, I was a 60-year-old greenhorn to the art of writing creative nonfiction. The serendipitous path that would eventually lead me to the DWC had its beginnings in 2010 with my breast cancer diagnosis. I picked up a pamphlet for the Y's Livestrong program, began participating, but needed to take a lengthy pause due to side effects of cancer treatments. Then I resumed Livestrong in 2014.

One day, I received an email invitation asking for submissions to an upcoming anthology of personal stories from breast cancer survivors. The project was a collaboration between the YMCA of Greater Syracuse's cancer support programs and the DWC. In January 2015, the DWC offered three Saturday workshops to help us novices get underway.

Months later, the anthology, ***Hopeful, Grateful, Strong: Survivor Stories***, was published. The Foreword and editing were by Linda Lowen, author and inspiring DWC instructor. The tranquil cover art of a single young sprout reaching skyward, was designed by Phil Memmer. When I had that book in hand and saw my name and essay in print within the bound pages, I felt an unexpected sense of personal worth and accomplishment, a milestone moment.

Since I was a teenager, I'd thought I should write a book about the troubles I'd been through. The events felt important to share, because maybe I could help empower other young women to avoid such dangers. I kept entries, some cryptic, in a locked diary. But the notion of ever writing those things down for others to read was too scary. Instead of sharing my stories, I carried them.

With the supportive atmosphere and messaging I found at the DWC in 2015, *write what you know, whatever your subject matter*, I signed up for The Flow, a critique-oriented class open to all skill levels. Finally, I began writing my stories. The DWC was where I received the reassurance and nudging that I needed to continue honing my evolving skills, and to keep going. The instructor, Georgia Popoff, was and still is paramount to the process with her encouragement to me and everyone, and is humble in saying, "Teach what you want to learn."

Years of classes and I keep writing, wondering when I'll be done. I have continued to be delightfully inspired (and a wee envious) as some fellow classmates have completed manuscripts and published their books. Among them is Apple An, a powerhouse of a woman with a gentle heart who writes captivating narratives about her journey from China to a new life in America.

Not long after publishing her first book, **Las Crosses**, Apple started this anthology collection with Georgia, intending it as an outlet for other writers to publish their short works. The first volume, **28 Voices**, included one of my pieces, "Worms." Again, I was thrilled to see my name and writing in print. Getting published is an acknowledgment of the hard work and such a satisfying feeling.

At the DWC, I learned from both instructors and students how to be a better writer. As my writing improved, it became more challenging because I expected more of myself and my work. Learning how to receive and give critique taught me more still, and I learned how to edit, edit, edit.

I could not have imagined when I first walked into the DWC that 10 years later I would be asked to write this Foreword for Volume II, **37 More Voices**, in the **Voices Heard Publishing Series**. I am honored.

Readers, if there's a part of your journey that is untold and feels important to tell, like the authors in this anthology, I hope you'll find your way to writing your story, too. Find your stride as a wordsmith and keep going.

# Introduction

## Apple An & Georgia A. Popoff

The YMCA of Central NY's **Downtown Writers Center** (DWC) opened its doors in 2001 to offer writing classes in all genres as the region's only literary center. DWC changed its name to **Writers Voice** in 2024.

Apple An started taking DWC classes in 2017 and benefited tremendously from the instructors and fellow writers over the next six years. They were instrumental in publishing her debut work (*Las Crosses*) in 2023. They also inspired her to find her calling as a storyteller to preserve what history overlooks, and to amplify the voices silenced by time and other factors.

As a way to contribute back to the services and the community, Apple decided to edit and publish collections of the writings by fellow writers from DWC/Writers Voice. In doing so, Apple hoped to

1. Offer writers a platform to share their own stories, to foster dialogue and understanding across cultures and times,

2. Benefit future programs offered by the Writers Voice with net proceeds from book sales, and

3. Encourage all writers to pay it forward by being generous with their time and effort to help promote each other's

work. Apple believes that in the literary world, a rising tide raises all boats.

The anthology idea became a reality after an animated brainstorming between Apple and Georgia A. Popoff, a DWC instructor since its beginning and program director since 2011, and the Onondaga County Poet Laureate.

In 2024, Voices Heard Publishing released ***28 Voices: A Nonfiction Anthology, Vol. 1***, a collection by authors who have studied in numerous classes at the **Writers Voice/DWC**. At the time, co-editors, Apple and Georgia, knew that one collection was insufficient to include many writers who have gathered in classrooms and on Zoom since the center started offering writing classes in the community. The editors also had the intention of encouraging many writers to continue sharing their stories in a future volume. Hence, this second volume of the ***Voices Heard Anthology Series***.

The call went out for submissions, and 46 writers responded. Of those, 37 pieces were selected, reviewed, edited, and finalized for this second collection. Readers can experience family stories, cherished memories, tales of survival, reflections on illness and healing, humor, and strength. Each author has given readers insight into their lives, hoping bridges can be built among readers and writers.

This is the power of writing and literature. Writers may first write to fulfill their own needs. At some point, they may want to share their writing with another. This step requires the writer to attend to many considerations in the structure, grammar, syntax, and even punctuation, to facilitate communication with a reader, to engage a reader, and to encourage them to keep reading. **Writers Voice** instructors provide guidance and knowledge of the elements of writing. The class experience facilitates friendship and mutual respect among the participants. With the focus on critique, a constructive and collaborative approach, rather than criticism, students receive feedback, learn from each other, and continue to develop their skills. They thrive, and so does their work that reflects their human experiences.

Bridges are built through the avenue of literature. Each of us is a unique individual whose stories matter. Perhaps a writer only wants to write to record a family history. Perhaps they have the goal of a book for publication. All reasons for writing and sharing are valid. In telling our stories in the form of memoir, a powerful genre and a noble endeavor, writers can connect with readers in a shared or similar experience. Illustrations of our diverse differences can offer information and knowledge, and give us reasons for compassion and empathy.

*37 More Voices*, along with *28 Voices,* presents to its readers many views of life as we know it. Congratulations to these 37 authors for writing their work, taking the courage to submit it for consideration, and for the publication in this collection. It is the editors' honor to offer the collection.

Congratulations, also, to the **Writers Voice** for 25 years of successful service, first as the only literary center in Central New York, and since COVID and with online instruction, now a community with people from throughout the United States and internationally.

The editors expect readers will gain much from each of these works. Thank you for supporting this work and all who created it.

# 1

## BUBBA

APRIL WILLIAMSON

"Applebee's Madison, how can I help you?" I say, sarcastically, into the phone at the end of the bar.

"Hey, my girl," coos Tiff, "how's work?"

"Same ol' shit." We gossip about coworkers for a few minutes. I hope I know the reason she's calling but I don't want to press her.

"Wanna have a girl's night tonight? Just you and me?"

"Hell yeah, I'll bring some beers."

We haven't had many girl's nights since she started dating Michael. I hope we're having one now because she finally dumped him.

I stop for beers on my way home to change. Tiff drinks vodka but I hate the stuff. It's nice out so I decide to walk over.

I've stayed the night at Tiff's so often she refers to her couch as my "sleepy couch" so I walk right in when I get there and lock the door behind me. She jumps up from the couch, trying to mask the distress on her face with a big smile as she comes over to hug me. She's already been drinking, her eyes are bleary. Bubba is excited to see me and is doing doggie dances, in and out of my legs, wagging his tail so hard it shakes his whole little body. He's a mutt, shaped like a wiener dog but thicker with long, soft hair. Tiff loves him like a child.

She gushes greetings at me in her sugary, sing-songy voice. "Oh, my girl. It's so good to see you. I can't believe it's been so long."

It usually annoys me when people talk in high-pitched tones to other adults, but with her it's so genuine, it doesn't bother me. She pulls me over to sit next to her on the couch and brushes her dyed, bright red hair back behind her ears in a nervous gesture. She's the sweetest person I've ever met and the urge to protect her overwhelms me at times.

I set my beers down on the floor beside the couch, pull one out, crack it open, and settle into the couch beside her. She asks more questions about one of our coworkers who's gotten herself into some juicy drama. I answer her questions but we both know why she wants me there and I'm waiting for her to get to the story.

"I left a message on his answering machine and told him I don't want to see him tonight."

I ask if something happened. She doesn't answer right away, which is not like her. I wait until she's ready to speak, slowly turning the beer bottle around in my hand, peeling the edges up ever so slightly as I go. I like to try and peel them off in one solid piece. The effort keeps me from chain smoking.

"I told him I wanted to have a girls' night and he got really upset. At first, he said he would miss me and was being sweet but I told him it would be okay and we'd see each other later and he started to get mad."

The first time he gave her a hard time about how much time she spends with friends, she told us, "He loves me so much, he just wants to spend time with me." And later, "He doesn't know how he'd live without me."

A couple of months into them dating, her mom came to visit and Michael balked at the idea of Tiff spending time with her alone. They went together to spend time with her but he was ready to leave after barely an hour. Her mom was so hurt that Tiff ended things with him. He promised to change and got her a puppy. Bubba was so little, with that long, soft hair. My heart fell when she showed up at my house with him the next day when Michael was at work. We'd only really seen each other at work in the weeks leading up to that visit. I was happy to see her but couldn't shake the feeling of discomfort about Bubba.

"When we hung up, he said he was coming over tonight and that was that. He's so mad all the time. I miss you, I miss everyone. But he was so angry and screaming at me. He said if I leave him, he's taking Bubba. Bubba is his dog." A tear slides down her cheek. "I told him it was fine, we could hang out tonight, but then I called back after he went to work and left the message. My phone's been off the hook since I called you. What am I going to do if he takes Bubba?"

Suddenly, Michael is pounding on the door. Tiff and I stare at each other, frozen in place. We both stand up when he takes a break. He resumes pounding and she walks toward the door. I head toward the bathroom with my beer.

Since I walked over, he has no way of knowing I'm here. I hear him yelling, then Bubba's shrill barking. She pleads with him to calm down.

I want to give them time to talk but the only thing I hear now is him screaming. I'm suddenly furious. I set my beer down on the counter in the bathroom, fling open the bathroom door, and storm down the hall to the kitchen. She's huddling in the corner, standing protectively in front of Bubba who is cowering behind her legs but still barking. I walk in behind them.

"He's my dog. I'm the one that got him. He's coming with me."

"Back away from her." He spins around.

"Mind your fucking business, bitch. What are you even doing here?"

"I was invited here, no one invited you, so get the fuck out."

He stares at me incredulously.

"Don't make me force you to leave."

He laughs. "How are you going to do that?"

I dash back to the bathroom, and he follows me, calling me a bitch again. I grab the beer I'd been drinking by the top and smash the bottom off on the edge of the sink. I lunge at him, slashing at his throat with the jagged edges of the bottle. The surprise and terror in his eyes thrills me.

"YOU BITCHES ARE BOTH CRAZY AS FUCK. I SHOULD CALL THE COPS ON YOU, YOU CRAZY ASS BITCH," he screams as he runs out the door.

"GO AHEAD, I DON'T GIVE A FUCK. SEND THE COPS, YOU CHICKEN SHIT ASS MOTHERFUCKER."

I stand in the doorway brandishing the broken bottle until his truck peels out of the parking lot.

I turn around and walk back into the apartment. Tiff looks stricken but relieved. She looks down at my hand and says, "Oh, you're bleeding."

I am bleeding profusely, still holding the jagged beer bottle, adrenaline coursing through me. She runs out of the room and comes back with a towel.

"I would have killed that motherfucker."

She startles me by laughing. "I know you would. He knew it, too!"

Now we're both laughing. She takes the broken beer bottle gingerly and gives me the towel to wrap my bloody hand in. I grab another beer and pace around the living room, still fuming. After a while she says. "I'm really done. I promise I'm not going back this time."

I plop back down next to her. Bubba lies between us on the couch, his head on Tiff's leg, watching us drink.

"Did you see his face?" We both laugh until we're crying.

A couple of mornings later, my phone rings until the machine picks up and then immediately starts to ring again. The second round of ringing jolts me all the way awake and I run to the phone. I've been waiting for this call.

"April, he took Bubba."

"Don't worry. We'll get him back."

"How? He says it's his dog and he'll have me arrested if I try to take him back."

"Come over. I'll figure it out while I get dressed."

She shows up in just enough time for me to brush my teeth, put on clothes, and shake off my hangover.

Tiff is a mess with mascara smeared on her face and her hair in clumps all over her head. She's usually so put together, seeing her like this enrages me.

"Did he take Bubba to his house?"

"I guess so. He won't answer his phone. I've called over and over. His roommate keeps hanging up on me."

"Stay here."

Michael lives down the street. There is a right turn at the end of my road that ends in a cul de sac, right next to the train tracks. I've often wondered how the people who live even closer than me to those tracks get any sleep. My mind strays absently to this thought again as I march down the street to get Tiff her dog back.

I walk straight up his driveway. Without bothering to knock, I try the door knob and it turns. I fling the door open and walk into the house without saying a word. Bubba runs right up to me and I scoop him up. Michael is standing there with his mouth hanging open. He doesn't say anything until I've turned and headed back toward the door.

"You crazy fucking bitch! How dare you walk into my house! Put my fucking dog down!"

I turn around when I get into the front yard and see him coming toward me. He's got at least 8 inches on me, probably 100 pounds, but he comes after me with a hammer. He swings it back in an arc over his head like he plans to bash mine in with it, right in his front yard.

"He's not your dog."

I look straight into his eyes. He's still holding the hammer over his head, ready to strike.

"Are you going to kill me with that thing?"

I see his eyes slide towards the next door neighbors who are standing in their driveway about 6feet away, staring at him in shock.

The absurdity of the situation strikes me. I throw my head back and laugh. I turn back around and walk away from him. The last thing I hear him say is that he's calling the cops.

I walk back up the street holding Bubba. Tiff is standing in my yard. She sees us and comes running to take Bubba from me. The look on her face makes the whole ordeal worth it.

"You saved him. Oh, my sweet Bubba, come to Mommy."

I suggest we take him inside to wait for the cops.

"What if they want to take him? We should hide him."

She puts a leash on Bubba and walks him around the side of my building, where the trash cans are stored. She pops Bubba into one of them and closes the lid.

"They'll never think to look in the trash."

I laugh. It might actually work.

We're still standing in the yard smoking when the officers roll up. They stop and slowly peel themselves out of the car.

"We don't have him," her voice is only a tiny bit shaky.

"Ma'am, we looked into it, and he has no dog registered in his name. As far as we're concerned, it's no one's dog and y'all need to figure this out on your own."

"Why did you come all the way here to tell us that?" I'd been expecting the cops to take his side.

"He sounded really angry and we weren't sure what was going on. He claims a crazy blonde woman walked into his house and took the dog. You don't know anything about that do you?"

"I sure don't."

"Okay, ma'am. Y'all stay safe."

They head back to the car. The one getting into the passenger side looks back over at us as he reaches for the door handle.

"Get that dog registered in your name immediately."

# 2

## SHUDDER

REN VANMEENEN

The taxi edges up to the curb in front of a tire shop. The front of the building is covered in rounds of rubber like a hypnotist's trick. This is a detail you want to remember. The man had gruffly instructed the driver to drop him off here and then take you across town. You are surprised when he pays the cab fare, but then again, he has taken all your money, instructed you to erase all the photos of him in your camera, kept you for hours after he did what he did. Now the man is sauntering off to find another drink. It is six in the morning, dusky. He leaves the car door open behind him as he stumbles out. You don't know the Turkish word for what he is, what he did, so you lean out and scream after him in English—just one noun that describes the only thing you know for sure about him. No one on the street seems to recognize the word, or care about a woman shouting after a man. You are sure he knows the word but he doesn't turn around. You feel the need to explain the situation to the taxi driver as he pulls out into traffic but all you can get out in his language is "Bad Man, Bad Man," pointing back to where you came from.

The taxi drops you off on the high road and you walk the labyrinthine streets downhill past scraggly stray cats to your apartment. Tomorrow you leave Istanbul to travel to the Black Sea. This is the last day of your summer here.

You walk up the three high flights to avoid the mirror in the elevator. You are relieved to find your roommates still asleep. You take a long, hot, scrubbing shower, ignoring the familiar advice about preserving physical evidence. You want there to be no trace.

You open your one window and throw the shutters wide, curl up on the bed as the sun rises higher. You close your eyes but your head spins. Pieces of the previous night start to come together. The mysterious call he made from the café at 2 AM—a conversation he knew you could not understand. A single guy with a closet full of children's clothing, little Velcro-strap shoes—blue and green and pink—lined up in the bathroom. A chain-smoker who doesn't own an ashtray. The power outage.

You cannot sleep. You don't cry. You call another American who has been living longer in this city. She meets you near the sea and you sit on a low curb to tell her your story. You are chain-smoking now too. She confirms what you assumed: in this mostly Muslim country all the blame will be on you. The bad man will walk away from any accusation as casually as he did from the taxi 2 hours before. If he was even who he said he was. If you could ever find him again.

You call the American Embassy anyway. You are told to go to the capital in Ankara, 5 hours southeast, to file a report. To become a statistic. You don't want to be just a number—you want to count. So you consider taking matters into your own hands—grabbing a cab, rushing across town, turning right at the tire store, going to the end of that long block, to the brown house on the corner of a narrow intersection, charging up to the second floor. Returning to the scene of the crime, this time in the daylight.

You know, however, that if you get in you might not be able to get out. The night before, when you had finally seen a chance to run, you had found the front door locked, the keyhole empty. You remember how he grabbed you from behind and spun you around, how he set his jaw, shook the key in your face, and pocketed it again. How he followed you back up the stairs, how he drained the last tall can of beer, how he continued to look at the floor, muttering about buying you dinner, how you owed him, how women always do this, how this was all your fault.

You will not change your plans. You will travel north. You will see a doctor when you get home just in case. She will find nothing of concern so you will try to forget. You will think of others—the bruised, the beaten, the lost. Like the woman from New York City found sprawled by the Istanbul railroad tracks a few months before you arrived. When the pillow was hovering over your face to muffle your screams, the stranger's taut body on top of yours, your first thought was of her. Then came the fast flash of images from the span of your own life consuming your vision—that old saw coming true.

But you survived. You will consider yourself one of the lucky ones. So you will do nothing, tell almost no one else. You will be there for others in their aftermaths without saying why. You will answer those calls, you will listen, you will witness, you will hold them up.

And your own eyes will—in time—stop fluttering when you sleep.

# 3

# JADE

SOPHIA TEJEIRO

My husband and I have a jade plant that sits in the north-west corner of our home. A decade ago, I inherited the plant from my mother, who needed a sunny spot to place it. That spot happened to be in one of my bedrooms.

I grew up in a 5-bedroom house, the youngest of four children. As the Omega, I didn't get my pick of rooms until my senior year of college, when I finally claimed all three on the second floor. One room was my study, another my bedroom, and the third a guest room.

My parents lived on the first floor. My mother's bad knees prevented her from climbing the stairs, and she appreciated my willingness to keep the upper rooms clean and tidy. Rather than embrace an empty nest, my parents encouraged me to stay home and save money until I could afford to move out, which, in their view, meant securing the financial stability of marriage, as my siblings had.

Once I commandeered the second floor, I switched bedrooms often depending on the dictates of Flying Star Feng Shui.[1] If it was predicted that inauspicious Chi would be in my southeast bedroom, I'd move to the northeast overnight, disassembling and reassembling my bed frame, lugging my nightstands and dressers across the hall. My office would migrate to the unlucky room, the jade following suit. The furniture stayed put until the energy shifted again the following month, demanding yet another rearrangement.

My mother, flabbergasted by my constant moving, called me crazy.

"Again?" she would question me. "What was wrong with the way you had it?"

"I don't like it anymore." Trying to explain further would only invite more criticism.

Feng Shui made its way into my life by chance. It was the summer of my junior year in college, and I was living in my parents' basement, heartbroken and unable to move on from my ex-boyfriend. I was looking through the bookshelves in the basement, feeling lost and hoping for answers when a bright red spine caught my eye: Home Design with Feng Shui A-Z. My curiosity piqued. I opened to a page that read: "If you want a change in your life, move 27 objects in your home."

That was my answer.

---

1. Flying Star Feng Shui is a school of Feng Shui that believes the energy within a home shifts based on the movement of celestial objects, known as flying stars. This energy changes annually in alignment with the Chinese New Year, but also fluctuates monthly, allowing practitioners to make continuous refinements to their living spaces. The goal of arranging a home according to Flying Star Feng Shui is to harness auspicious energy while minimizing the effects of negative influences.

The next day I made plans to move out of the stagnant Chi in the basement. Agency and purpose entered my life again: transform my room into a sanctuary, and good fortune would follow. I threw out the boring, old bed frame I inherited and replaced it with one that had a headboard adorned with decorative curls, reminiscent of Cinderella's pumpkin carriage. To have balanced Chi while I slept, I needed nightstands on each side of my bed with matching lamps to anchor the Chi. The perfect nightstands appeared at a garage sale and matching lamps were easy to find at IKEA. Lastly, to ensure the Chi remained grounded, I needed a dresser to face the foot of my bed. Going to estate sales every weekend, I eventually found an antique dresser from 1910 in an elderly woman's basement. It needed to be stripped of paint, but it was only 10 dollars, and I had more time than money to spend making my bedroom a sanctuary.

Chi and Chaos are important concepts to understand when practicing Feng Shui. Chi is energy, it is in everything, it is ever-changing, and wants to flow. Chaos is one way that energy arranges itself and can be positive or negative. Active Chaos is birthing energy and necessary for life; you can feel it when you're passionate and swept up in the creative process. Passive Chaos, on the other hand, is draining and results in stagnant Chi. You can feel it when you look at clutter or the mess you can't bring yourself to clean up.

At the peak of my college heartache, I was drowning in Passive Chaos. The basement was dark, and the dehumidifier buzzed incessantly. The bookshelves were filled with forgotten English anthologies and photo albums. The one closet housed even more photos strewn about in boxes. In the back corner, my sister's wedding dress hung yellowing with time, and on the shelves sat unopened bottles of tequila, rum, and scotch my father received as gifts from patients, colleagues, and friends.

Like my surroundings, the memories of the breakup remained untouched and spoiling.

"Just tell me you don't love me anymore."

He wouldn't.

"Say it."

It took him a long time. We walked up and down my street, and it seemed like for those moments we stepped out of the time pendulum. I wasn't sure if he was stalling or working up the courage to say goodbye.

Finally, he said it: "I don't love you."

The timbre of his voice sounded as if he were breaking his own heart.

I half smiled. My heart armored up to protect itself from further heartbreak. I said goodbye and quietly walked away.

My rash and cold response caused more suffering than necessary. I couldn't let go of the sense of betrayal and abandonment I felt. At the time, I lacked the experience to see that we simply weren't compatible—that no one was to blame. And so, the heartache lingered for years. When Feng Shui promised that moving out of the basement might bring happiness, restful sleep, and even love again, I needed to believe it.

I gravitated toward Feng Shui because of a lifelong anxiety that I was not good enough. I'd already been practicing yoga and Buddhism to help with my stress up until that point.

It started in middle school with Wai Lana Yoga on PBS; for 30 minutes I could escape my adolescent angst and just learn new ways to move my body. While my parents and siblings slept, I was practicing headstands by the blue light of the TV at 6 AM. Wai Lana was teaching me to be confident, regardless of my poor hand-eye and foot-eye coordination, which made me dread gym class. By my sophomore year of college, I had graduated to hot yoga and dabbled with Ashtanga. I felt physically empowered—strong without being athletic, grounded without needing a plan for my future.

But the physical challenge of yoga, while helpful in easing the physiological symptoms of anxiety, couldn't touch the grief of my breakup. I needed more than movement—I needed someone to hold my hand and guide me through healing. My friends kept telling me to "just let go," but none of them could tell me how to do it.

Desperate for instructions, I searched for meditations on letting go, and stumbled upon Audio Dharma. The podcast's library of Dharma talks was seemingly infinite. I didn't have to study in a Zen Buddhist monastery to learn about the Eightfold Path. The teachers had already traveled the world, studying various Buddhist traditions, and they shared their wisdom for free. Their guidance helped me sit with my emotions and become less reactive to them. But while meditation offered a way to be with my heartache, it didn't promise immediate relief. Grief wasn't something that could be unraveled in a 20-minute seated practice.

The little red book, on the other hand, promised I could transform my pain—all I had to do was rearrange some furniture.

I developed a practice that wove Feng Shui and Dharma together, a fusion that helped ease my anxiety about love. Designing my environment according to prescribed rules, while learning about the Four Noble Truths, gave me something to focus on—something to keep my hands busy and my mind at ease. I felt protected: too occupied with organizing and cleansing my space, I had no time to create more bad karma for myself.

The combination of both practices became a kind of moving meditation. As I perfected my environment, I believed I was perfecting my mind. Being so good and perfect, no one would be able to break my heart again was my underlying belief. And when I wanted something to change in my life, I could just move another 27 items in my home. I hadn't learned to apply the principles of Feng Shui to people in my life yet, nor to hold others up to the same Buddhist precepts I was striving toward myself.

While Feng Shui is a philosophy of home design, it is also a practice in self-awareness. It demands an honest look at yourself and what you truly value: Does everything you surround yourself with bring you joy? Do you love every object in your environment?

These principles extend beyond material possessions to the people in your life. My desire to be good—to strive for perfection—had shaped my character, but it had also kept me from setting healthy boundaries in relationships.

When my mother gave me the jade, she told me it was a money plant in Feng Shui. Later, I learned that where you place it in your home influences how finances flow into or out of your life. Each cardinal and ordinal direction carries a specific Chi, and the jade's placement in any of these directions can help boost the financial energy associated with it.

The first day I adopted the jade, I over-watered it. Thinking I could dry out the soil, I placed it next to an electric heater and left it there. When I returned, the right side was scorched and drooping. I thought I had killed it. Despite my initial neglect, the jade survived.

It grew taller, its stem thickening into a woody trunk, and I was able to take clippings that grew into new shoots.

Living with my parents rent-free, my financial situation wasn't urgent, but I still longed for a change—enough of a change to leave. Unfortunately, that wasn't in the cards. While under their roof, I took out student loans for a master's degree. During this time, the jade grew, maturing alongside the weight of my student loans. I learned that my debt was halting my progress, and much like my living situation, it felt like there was nothing I could do to change it—except rearrange some furniture.

Since my junior year of college, I've faithfully practiced Feng Shui. By the time I met my husband 8 years later, I had come to understand the resilience and generosity of my jade plant. After several months of dating, I gave him a clipping, hoping it would ease his financial worries. It worked. He found a better job and a side gig teaching the martial art, Muay Thai.

A year later, we moved in together, bringing our jades with us. The better care we gave them, the more our finances flourished. We paid off debts, built an emergency fund, and eventually got married. As part of our wedding ritual, we reunited the once-separated clippings in a single planter.

Now, we nurture the jade plant together. My husband, grounded and steady, helps anchor my anxieties before they spiral. And for the first time in years, I've stopped rearranging furniture incessantly.

**4**

# THIS FAMILY HAS TIES TO THE MAFIA

FRANCESCA SWICK

My severe allergy to sports was self-diagnosed in my adolescence. When I met my husband Eli, he understood quickly that I was not a sports girl. He would occasionally watch an NFL or NHL game on his phone, but in the early days of our relationship he neither tried to convert me nor took too much of our time together for sports. I loved that he didn't care about college basketball, a phenomenon that had plagued me every March growing up in Syracuse, NY. Then two things happened. We got married, and he fell back into the rhythm of being a Bills fan. He started to need to watch every Bills game...and the games that affected the Bills games, which was, according to my calculations, *all of them*.

I reverted to my childhood coping mechanisms to deal with this. On game days we would spend time together until the game started, and then I'd make my escape to the bedroom during those 4-hour stretches. I'd catch up on reading, play Animal Crossing on my Nintendo Switch, and watch movies he wasn't interested in. When he sweetly begged me to watch the game with him, I would only make it a few minutes in before my eyes would glaze over and I'd start to think about what else I could be doing with my precious Sunday. Football was boring.

Then there was the Mafia of it all. For the uninitiated, the Buffalo Bills call their fans the "Bills Mafia." My understanding of the Mafia came exclusively from Martin Scorsese films and ABC's daytime soap opera *General Hospital*. As a woman of Italian heritage, I grew up quite separated from my Italian culture, so witnessing these depictions felt like discovering a piece of my own history. Though my family certainly wasn't involved in the Mob, something about these portrayals felt familiar and comforting, *Goodfellas* in particular. The characters often had the same Brooklyn accent as my Grandfather. They were dedicated to each other, would kill or die for each other if necessary, and it often was. Sure, they were gritty, violent and hypermasculine, but they were also capable of prepping the tomato sauce first before taking care of business. I recognize that not all Italian-Americans appreciate these stereotypes, but the American Mob in Scorsese's filmography always felt to me like a chosen family, just with more casualties. Maybe this is why I initially balked at the "Bills Mafia." The NFL couldn't co-opt that language for football of all things. My father-in-law, a Bills fan since childhood, ignored my teasing as he resolutely stuck his Bills-themed sign in the front yard each September when the season began. "This Family Has Ties to the Mafia," the sign reads, a red and blue buffalo stamped below the text.

In 2021, I had the idea to get my husband tickets to a game as an early Christmas present. He was delighted, and in my mind I had secured the Best Wife Award for this noble sacrifice. In mid-December, bundled in our winter gear and Buffalo merch, we made the 2-hour drive to Orchard Park. Though I was apprehensive, we had a blast. It filled me with joy to see Eli so happy, and I cheered hesitantly, wanting to fit in but not knowing how to give myself over to the Bills mania. I was intoxicated by the energy of the crowd and the camaraderie between us all. Every time the Bills scored a touchdown, the loudspeakers blared the song, "Shout," and at the top of their lungs the entire stadium began singing, "The Bills make me want to SHOUT!" This was mind-blowing to me, as someone who believed the sensitivity of the arts was not in harmony with the world of sports. The Bills beat the Panthers (31-14), and I was tentatively entranced, high-fiving and befriending strangers next to me. I didn't yet call myself a Bills fan, chalking it up to a fluke.

2022 was a difficult year for us, and the hardships came to an abrupt end on a Friday evening in December. The next morning, Eli woke up and said, "We could get two tickets to the game tomorrow for under $300."

"Do it," I replied in an instant. This spontaneity was a rush.

What delighted me that time wasn't even the game. It was the community we found in the parking lot tailgate beforehand. We met up with one of my oldest friends from high school and his wife, who had moved to Buffalo and had season tickets. Like the good Italian woman I am, I showed up to their tailgate with Wegmans cannoli dip. We ate burgers and pulled pork sandwiches that were surprisingly delicious, considering they had been cooked in a parking lot. It was a chilly, drizzly day, and after consuming a respectable amount of alcohol, we all teetered through a shortcut that would get us to the stadium in minutes rather than miles. There was something sweet about tipsy people helping other tipsy people across a slippery creek-bridge in the woods.

That game, the Bills defeated the Jets (20-12) and I was 100 feet away as Josh Allen hurdled over a linebacker to land a first down. The energy of the crowd was infectious, and I screamed my lungs out along with them, despite the fact that Eli was away at the concession stand.

About a year later in 2023, Eli was talking about the Bills with a customer at the coffee shop he manages when they asked, "Do you wanna go to the Dolphins game?"

Used to customers sometimes being a little too familiar with him, Eli jokingly replied, "Not with you."

It turned out that this customer had been offered a pair of tickets to the Bills-Dolphins game for the weekend of October 1st, in the "Club" section. This, I learned later, is sports speak for Fancy. He did not care to go to the game, so he offered the tickets to Eli. Ironically, the weekend before Eli received this offer, we had actually gotten in a fight about the Bills, because it felt like football had become more important than us spending time together. When Eli came home from work that day, he was sheepish.

"Listen, this is going to be ironic given our weekend, but…"

The moment he was done explaining that we had two free tickets to the game in 2 weeks, I laughed out loud.

"Hell yeah! Of course we're going."

The feeling of community was palpable in the streets of Buffalo as we drove to the game on a warm and sunny October day. Folks lined the sidewalks with grills and coolers, gathering with friends and family. We laughed as we drove by a man sitting on a sidewalk bench with a party-sized box of Goldfish crackers and disposable plastic cups screaming, "Goldfish! Goldfish for all my friends!" We hypothesized that he was looking out for the people who were likely to drink too much that day.

That time, we did it right. We got there early, parked in our *free* parking space included with our tickets and began the tailgate, toasting the rich, retired doctor we had to thank for our seats. We met up with my old friend again, and had a great time chatting with them on the way into the stadium. We were just settling in to our Club seats, when over the loudspeaker I heard,

"Where else would you rather be than right here, right now?"

I was thunderstruck.

"...nowhere," I answered aloud, awed by my own feelings in that moment.

After all this time and all this avoidance of football, here I was, watching an NFL game and happy—no, *delighted*—to be there. Eli laughed at my reaction.

"You haven't heard that before? That's like... their thing."

These words, spoken by former Buffalo Bills head coach Marv Levy, became the heart song of the team and its fan base when he first uttered them in 1986. He recited these words of serenity to his team before every game throughout his tenure as coach. Since then, they've begun playing a recording of Marv delivering these words over the loudspeaker in the stadium at the start of every home game. Something about this made me emotional. It could've been because I was drunk, but these words felt familiar to me, like a powerful meditative mantra. The idea that the head coach of an NFL team would call his players into a moment of mindfulness before each game was moving to me.

The Bills crushed the Dolphins (48-20), and I did my part by singing and screaming "Let's go Buffalo!" and "Hey-ey-ey-ey" when instructed. I befriended the drunk woman in front of me based on our matching Bills scrunchies, and heard her life story. She grew up in Buffalo and was a die-hard Bills fan, but lived in Miami with her Dolphins fan husband. Every year they go to two games, one in Buffalo and one in Miami. I listened to her as though it were a groundbreaking episode of *Oprah*. The Bills were up at this point, her husband slumped in his seat beside her.

Before this, I didn't quite understand the Bills Mafia. They get drunk and break tables, so what? But that day, at that game, I got it. The Bills Mafia isn't just a name for the fans. They are an entity not dissimilar to the American Mafia, in that they're a family. And if you're there, you're part of it. Still, I remained hesitant to call myself a Bills fan. Are you really a fan if you only watch the games at the stadium?

In 2024, I watched the last game of the season from beginning to end on the couch with my husband. The game was at home in Buffalo against quarterback Patrick Mahomes and the Kansas City Chiefs. My heart was in it so much more than I anticipated, my entire body tense. When the cameras showed Taylor Swift, who is currently dating the Chief's tight-end Travis Kelce, in the stadium I'd visited three times before, something snapped in me. I felt territorial. *Get out of our house!* I thought. And then, *wow, I've fully lost it.* That game was a devastating, late game loss, and the one where I became a Bills fan.

What I've learned from years of being a Buffalo onlooker is that being a fan doesn't mean only loving them at their best. It means loving them through their losses, and putting the sign in the front yard every year, no matter what. Quarterback Josh Allen has famously said that he will never leave the team, that he simply isn't interested in going to the Super Bowl with anyone but Buffalo. This is the mark of a true Bills fan. There's something valiant about staying dedicated to the team through their lower moments. *I've been here. I loved them even when things didn't look so good.* This is a badge of honor to the members of the Bills Mafia. It's burying the body in the middle the night in middle of nowhere Upstate New York in the pouring rain. It's not pretty, but you do it because it has to be done.

My husband has taught me to love many unexpected things over the course of our relationship. Tomatoes. The occasional Guinness. The music of John Prine. *Seinfeld*. But none more surprising than the Buffalo Bills. I now own my fair share of Bills merch, including a tee shirt that is the pièce de résistance. It features a photo of Josh Allen and former Bills wide-receiver Stefon Diggs photoshopped into a scene in *Goodfellas*, channeling Ray Liotta and Joe Pesci cackling joyfully. Below the image is a play on the opening line of *Goodfellas*, "As far back as I can remember, I always wanted to be a Bills fan." These days, I look at my father-in-law's sign in the front yard fondly. This family does have ties to the Mafia.

# 5

## THREES AND FIVES ARE WILD

### JACKIE SOUTHARD

"Ryan, Scott, I want you to meet Heather. She'll be your sitter for tonight."

Ryan and Scott, 7 and 5, were good kids. But they were not easy. Their high levels of energy and creativity tend to get them into trouble. We needed someone that would pay attention to them. There would be no downtime, the boys wouldn't go to bed until we got home, and the sitter would have to be their playmate. Not many sitters have those specific qualifications.

Joyce, our neighbor and friend, knew the boys, how active they were, and how hard it was to find a sitter. One day, we were outside enjoying a usually warm October day, watching the brilliant red, orange, and yellow leaves float to the ground.

"I may have found a babysitter for you," Joyce said. "Her name is Heather, and she lives right around the corner. She's great with kids. I think she would be a good fit for Ryan and Scott."

After our conversation, I made a beeline for the phone and called Heather, asking if she was available Saturday night. She said yes and would love to sit for us. Yay, I thought.

Heather arrived on time, and after a quick tour of the house and an overview of their routines, we walked into the kitchen.

"This is Ryan," I said. I pointed toward Ryan, who paced around the kitchen table, grabbing a chicken nugget as he passed his seat. His eyes were glued to a Goosebumps book. He raised his hand holding the nugget, gave a little wave, and took a bite. There was no eye contact.

Scott, apprehensive about a new babysitter, half-sat on the chair with one leg curled under him and one foot on the floor, making it easy to pop up and down throughout dinner.

"And this is Scott," I said. Scott held a nugget as he sipped his milk. With a sideways glance, he whispered, "Hi."

Heather walked over and sat in the seat next to him, "Hi, Scott. I'm Heather. How are you?" Scott just looked at her with questioning eyes, unsure what to make of her. "That looks good. What are you eating?"

"Chik'n nuggets."

"They're my favorite."

"Mine, too," he said, and a smile crossed his face.

It was then I knew she would be perfect for them.

That evening, we arrived home at nine. I heard voices in the kids' room and went upstairs. Heather sat on the floor reading *Are You My Mother* aloud while Ryan and Scott, in their Teenage Mutant Ninja Turtles pajamas, squirmed and rolled around. They all laughed as they debated, "Who was the bird's mother? Was the kitten, the dog, or Snort, the backhoe?"

"Hi everyone," I said.

"Hi, Mom," the boys replied. They didn't look up but continued their debate as they started performing somersaults.

"Hi, Mrs. Southard," Heather said as she stood up. "They were really good. After dinner, we played some card games and rode bikes. They wanted to build a fort from the couch cushions, but I suggested the bike ride instead."

"That would have been okay. They love to rearrange the sectional and pillows. There are blankets downstairs you can use, too." I turned toward the boys, "Okay, guys, hop into bed. I'll be back in a minute."

Both boys hopped across the floor, laughing. She giggled at their antics. I took a deep breath and smiled. This was going to work out great.

Heather babysat for us for a few years, and when she wasn't available, we'd ask Amy or Sarah, Heather's best friends. All three girls were focused on the boys, doing activities, playing games, or bike riding. One evening, Heather asked if it would be okay if Amy and Sarah came over and babysat with her.

"They like playing with the boys, too," she said, "and they don't want to get paid."

"Sure," I said, thinking six eyes were better than two. "That would be fun for the boys, too," I replied.

That evening, the three girls arrived at the front door with wide grins; all wore their hair in ponytails and donned puffy ski jackets with colorful scarves wrapped around their necks. I smiled; it reminded me of my friends from school. The comradery, wearing the latest style of clothes, which for us were bell bottom hip-hugger jeans, tie-dyed t-shirts that we made, and our long straight hair that flowed down to our waists.

"Come on in, girls," I said. We walked into the kitchen where the boys were playing cards. "Ryan and Scott, guess what? We have *three* sitters for you tonight."

They looked in my direction and saw Heather, Amy, and Sarah waving at them.

Scott jumped up. "Yay," he said, waving at them.

"Come on, we're playing cards," Ryan said as he gathered the cards. "You can play too."

"Threes and fives are wild," Scott added.

"Threes and fives are wild?" Heather repeated with a giggle. "What kind of game is that?"

"You'll see," Ryan said.

The girls took a seat at the table, leaning in to listen as Scott rambled on about how to play this made-up version of a card game.

Mike looked at me, nodding his head toward the door. "Looks like we're good to go."

I nodded and turned toward the kids. "Hey, guys, we're heading out now." We said goodbye, and they all waved as the cards were dealt.

When Mike and I returned a few hours later, we heard laughter from the family room downstairs.

"We're home," Mike yelled loud enough so they could hear us.

"Sounds like they're having fun," I said.

We walked over to the top of the opened staircase that led to the family room downstairs. We saw two pairs of legs and two sets of feet across one of the steps, indicating that the boys were hanging upside down. Mike and I faced each other and shrugged.

"What are they doing now?" Mike asked.

"Who knows," I said.

"We're downstairs," Heather yelled. "We're playing charades."

We descended the stairs, stepped around the legs, and entered the family room. The girls faced Ryan and Scott, hanging upside down, side-by-side, with their arms folded in front of them. Their blond hair hung straight down, and t-shirts gathered around their armpits exposing their ribs. Their heads were 3 feet above the floor.

"Hi, Mrs. Southard," the girls said in unison. They bounced up and down, and their ponytails swayed back and forth.

"Guess what we are," Scott yelled.

"Are you a gymnast?" Amy said.

"No," the boys cried out.

"Awww."

"Fruit?"

"Ha ha ha, no."

"Are you an animal?"

"Yes."

"A snake? A bird? A monkey?" The girls threw out every animal that could think of. They were so quick with their guesses that Mike and I had no time to answer.

"No, not even close," Ryan exclaimed.

"What are you then?"

"We're bats," the boys screamed. Then they unfolded their arms, flapped their bat wings, and squeaked.

"Hahahaha," the girls' shrieked. Their cheeks red from laughter.

"We love watching your kids," Heather said.

"They are so funny," Amy added.

"Yes, they are," Mike said.

The boys pulled themselves up, slid their legs from between the steps, and dropped to the floor.

Mike and I went upstairs, and the boys and girls followed behind, chatting about the game.

"Should we pay all three?" Mike whispered.

"I think so. They're great, and they keep the boys entertained."

After that, we often hired all three to sit for the boys.

The following spring, Mike and I had a dinner to attend, a birthday surprise for a friend. Heather watched the boys. When we returned, we entered the mudroom, slipped our boots off, and hung our coats in the closet. Heather, Ryan, and Scott's voices drifted in from the living room.

"We're home," I called out as we entered the kitchen, and then I saw two blue blankets hanging from the balcony in the living room; it looked like two teardrops hovering 5 feet off the floor. The blankets moved, and voices echoed from within.

I took a sharp breath and whispered, "Mike, Mike, look!" I nudged his side with my elbow. Mike looked up. We ran to the living room.

"Hey, Mom, Dad," the boys yelled.

"Look at us," Ryan yelled.

"We're cocoons," Scott said. Two sets of blue eyes peeked over the top of their cocoons.

"What are you guys doing? You could get hurt," Mike said, his voice distressed. We stood beside the cocoons and stretched our arms underneath them in case they fell.

Heather sat on the steps and grinned from ear to ear, her ponytail draped over her shoulder. "They must be really creative to think of these things," she said, smiling.

"Yeah, they're creative, alright," I chuckled.

Scott pushed his hand out of the cocoon and pointed to the balcony above. "We won't get hurt, the blankets are tied around the railing,"

"The ends are tucked under the knots, and our weight presses on it, so it won't come loose," Ryan added.

Mike looked at me and whispered, "I'm going upstairs to check." I nodded.

"Guys, how did you get in there?" I asked.

"We got on the table and climbed in," Scott said.

"They're okay," Heather added with confidence and a slight nod, "I checked the knots upstairs. They're really tight."

"Okay," I replied. I believed her, but glad that Mike went to double-check.

"We've been playing a riddle game," Heather continued. "They have some really hard ones."

Both boys ducked back into their cocoons. "Okay, Mom, Dad, guess this. It's as light as a feather, but the strongest man in the world can't hold it for 3 minutes," Scott said.

"I don't have any idea," I replied, unsure if we should play this game or get them down.

"Me either," Mike said as he walked down the stairs. As he reached me, he leaned in and softly said, "The knots are fine." Then he looked at the cocoons, then me, and shook his head in disbelief. I relaxed and backed away from the cocoons.

"At least they're safe," I added.

"Your breath. You can't hold your breath for 3 minutes," Scott yelled.

"Good one, Scott," I replied as I lingered near the cocoons, just in case.

"Mom, Dad," Ryan yelped, "guess this one. An airplane crashed on the border between two countries. Where are the survivors buried?"

"You got me. I don't know. Where?" I asked.

"In their hometown," Mike said as he gave Heather a wink, indicating he knew the answer. The boys burst into laughter.

"They're not buried! Survivors aren't dead," Ryan said.

"You have to be *dead* to be *buried*," Scott laughed.

"Another good one," Mike said.

Heather piped in, "They've been in the cocoons for over an hour."

"Really? Over an hour?"

"Yup, they like it in there."

"Mike, did you hear that?"

"Yeah, over an hour," he echoed, still apprehensive about the cocoons.

"You know, Mike," I said. "They *stayed still* in one place for *more than 5 minutes*. Maybe we should consider using the cocoons."

Mike looked at me from the corner of his eye and said, "Really?!"

"No. I'm kidding," I added, then said to the boys, "Come on, guys, let's get you out of there and up to bed."

The boys poked their heads out of the top of the cocoons, arms raised. Mike and I grabbed them and lifted them out of their cocoons while Heather helped pull the blankets off the boys' legs and feet.

"Okay, guys. Up you go," I said.

The boys gave Heather a hug and waved goodbye. "See you later!" they yelled as they turned and hopped up each step until they reached the landing.

Mike and I looked at each other and smiled, knowing that the boys were happy and safe, the sitters were enjoying themselves with the boys, and now, when we go out, we can sit back and relax.

**6**

## GHOST MOTHER

### DYANA SMOLEN

It's nighttime, and I am chasing her from the living room, past the front door, up the wide wooden staircase to the darkened upper landing. I call out to her—"Mommy, wait! Mom!" but she disappears into the black void at the top of the stairs.

I close my eyes and see her still—gliding up the stairs, silken housecoat billowing behind her like fluttering sheets hung out on a breezy summer day. I am right behind her, but she is unaware. Or does she know I am there? Is my mother running from me?

I dreamed this dream when I was young, around 7, I think. But even after five decades, the memory of the dream is clear, its meaning still potent—making my throat tighten, my heart ache. The central figure in my life disappeared. Where did my mother go?

The home we shared was centuries old, a 5-bedroom farmhouse that served as the backdrop of my childhood, my mother's and her father's, as well. At one point, it was beautiful, made from dark, solid wood with a wraparound porch and a large dry goods storage room at the back that was rumored to have been a store for travelers of the old Erie Canal. As family lore would have it, the hardy voyagers would disembark, walk from the towpath over a footbridge, and stretch their legs for several hundred feet along a narrow path to our house and back.

When I was young, there were three bodies of water running behind the house—the old Erie Canal, also known as Clinton's Ditch, the Erie Canal, and the Mohawk River—as well as railroad tracks that followed a similar path. A steel truss railroad bridge spanned the Mohawk River, allowing trains to travel East to West, and vice versa, carrying goods and people from one end of New York State to the other. When we were still in elementary school, my brother, cousins, and I would follow the paths to the tracks, against our parents' wishes, and hide in the tall weeds, so close we could feel the rumbling of the trains in our bones.

One summer, we heard the adults talking in hushed tones. A group of teenagers had been drinking on the train tracks, they said, and one had passed out on the bridge. When the train struck, one young man was cut in half—part of his trunk remaining on the platform above, while the other splashed into the muddy water below. For months after the accident, I would make my way to the bridge, propelled by a macabre fascination to look for bodily remains.

When I was 5, my parents moved into the house after my grandparents relocated to a rustic cabin in the Adirondacks, a move that would see my grandmother dead within the year. For some reason, I had chosen the front room of the house as my bedroom, its double windows overlooking the road and a large red barn that had since gone derelict. In my grandfather's time, the property had been a working farm operated primarily by the boys of the family under the austere direction of their father, a preacher who was more invested in saving souls than tending to the needs of his family. By the time we moved in, the only evidence of the long-ago homestead was the barn, its roof collapsing, the smell of long-gone hay still pungent inside its buckling walls.

My bedroom was oversized for a small child. Despite a single bed, dresser, and lamp, there was a large play area that could fit another set of everything. At the foot of my bed, next to the door, a small two-shelf metal bookcase held my favorite Dick and Jane books, along with picture books and tomes filled with words I could not yet read. At that time, there was no overhead lighting in the room, only plug-in desk lamps to illuminate the space after sunset. Four of us lived in the residence at the time and the rooms of my older brother and parents felt miles away on the other side of the house.

One night, as I was lying on my back half asleep in the darkened bedroom, an apparition appeared. At the doorway was a tall, thin male figure, all shades of gray and silver, moving slowly forward and stopping in front of the window. After a moment, he silently turned and looked toward me, at which point I frantically pulled the blanket over my head and screamed bloody murder.

"MOOOOOOOOOOMMMM!     MOOOOOOOOOOM-MMM!"

It took forever for my half-asleep mother to stumble into my room and turn on my bedroom light.

"What is it? What's wrong?" she asked, fully annoyed that I had awoken her.

"It was a ghost! I saw a ghost!" I cried hysterically.

"There's no such thing as ghosts," my mother replied. "You were just dreaming. Now go back to sleep."

"Can I sleep with you?" I begged, afraid to be in that room or anywhere in that house, for that matter, alone.

"No," she said, dismissively. "I have to work in the morning."

After clicking off the lamp, she closed the door and shuffled down the hall to the other end of the house. I lay in that small bed, trembling in fear. If the ghost returned, I was on my own, that much was clear.

Years later, before the barn across the road was torn down, I found a photo of my grandfather's father and mother. It was a tattered black-and-white image in a pile of yellowed papers. When I picked up the photo, I recognized the face of the man. It was my great-grandfather, my ghostly visitor.

As an adult fast approaching my senior years, I still vividly recall the dream of my mother gliding away from me on the staircase, disappearing into darkness. And I can still see the silvery silhouette of my great-grandfather, tall and thin, floating across my room. Even now, I am haunted by the rupture of disconnection and the deep sense of aloneness I felt in that house, which left me endlessly chasing safety, love, and acceptance—all of it still just beyond my reach.

# 7

## GIVING

### LISA MARIE SELLIN

My mother's anger is normally silent and chilly. She will act hurt, injured, simmer with it, answer all questions with short sarcastic utterances. Somehow all actions my siblings and I take in life come back to how it impacts her.

Even now as a dementia patient her true character emerges. Recently, I was visiting her at her memory care facility, telling her about the house I bought last year.

"You used my money for that?"

"No, I used my money."

"Hmmph."

No questions about the house or where it was. Some things I have to let go at this point.

In 1994, when I told my parents I had matched someone in the bone marrow donor registry and began explaining the steps of the procedure, my mother became dramatic in her rage and sadness.

"Why are you doing this?"

My mother's forearms and hands flapped up and down. I calmly explained that part of my motivation was to help someone else with a terminal disease.

"If Mike had had the same opportunity, if someone could have helped him...."

Mike was one of my two brothers. He had died 3 years earlier at age 31 from lung cancer. Getting registered as a possible marrow donor seemed like a meaningful action to take while I was still dealing with his death. Bereft describes my feelings at watching my brother's illness progress for the 2 years he lived with it. Helpless was an oft felt emotion during that time when so few treatment options were available to him. I had been living in Thailand for several years after college; he was diagnosed with cancer only a year after my return. It seemed we'd only been adults to each other for a short time.

"But why do you have to do this?"

I assumed my mother felt that I was taking unnecessary risks, but she never quite said those words. She was bothered that I was putting "them" (my parents) through all this. My father sat in his recliner on the other side of the room and gazed away from us.

"The National Marrow Donor Program (NMDP) office told me that the procedure takes about an hour and that they'll be checking on my health leading up to it."

I thought it would help to share what I knew about the marrow donation, when it would be, what I should expect in terms of my condition on leaving the hospital. In the briefing the NMDP gave me no one ever said, "Your mother might be angry that you're doing this."

After my attempt at conversation with my mother weeks before the harvest (donation), she gave me a sullen silent treatment, a typical way for her to deal with conflict of any kind.

The NMDP first notified me that I was a match in mid-March. The marrow harvest was scheduled for the Thursday before Memorial Day. I realized as the time grew closer that I had to be careful about getting sick or getting into an accident. For the patient this would be detrimental or worse. Whenever I drove on a highway, whenever I felt myself rushing to do anything, I had to remind myself to be more cautious.

When I first got the phone call while at work, I was shaking, but I was thrilled. I was sitting at my desk in a large room filled with individual cubicles, each with 6 feet high beige textile walls.

The usually noisy room went quiet.

It was exciting to be matched as it meant I would be useful and not just be languishing on the registry for years. I was anxious to share with my colleagues that I was a possible match to someone.

I had learned about becoming a donor from a department newsletter which highlighted another colleague's marrow donation some months before. He worked in the Data Center, in another building on campus and I didn't know him but having been a blood donor myself, this drew my interest. A vintage car enthusiast group sponsored a bone marrow registration drive; when I saw the flyers posted for it in our cafeteria, I signed up.

I saw marrow donation as something to do for someone else that would help cure them of a disease. I thought of my brother, Mike, and his lung cancer and how he had searched for all possibilities of a cure. My participation inspired at least one friend to get on the marrow registry after I donated. Another friend donated blood for the first time in her late 40s.

In late May on a late afternoon I checked into the hospital. I got settled in my double room. During my stay my cousin, Mary Lou, my Uncle Ray, and my sister, Khris visited me.

A couple I knew, Mary and Drew, came to the hospital twice.

"Hey, Sellinoid, what's the deal? We came earlier and you were MIA!"

Drew thought it was hilarious that I had left the building. The hospital staff gave me a 2-hour pass at dinner time. As a healthy person, I wasn't required to be constantly monitored through the evening but needed to be ready to go at dawn. Khris and I had dinner at King David's before rushing back to the boredom of the grey walls at Upstate Hospital. No one had missed me yet.

My father phoned me that night at the hospital.

"I'm sorry I'm not up there to visit, but I'm thinking about you. I hope everything goes well tomorrow."

I was awake for a while after that, wondering how upset my mother was.

Early the next morning, hospital staff brought me to surgery. The procedure took about an hour, followed by recovery. There was some pain at the harvest points (where a large needle was inserted into my buttocks). The only evidence afterwards was surgical tape on my lower back and pain deep at the wound site. I was very tired throughout the day and slept a lot.

A nurse in recovery told me my father had been in the waiting area during my procedure and left once he knew I got through it ok. Mary Lou is a nurse and she was attentive in her visit. Uncle Ray came by my bed and patted my arm, rubbed my shoulder gently.

The marrow donation procedure is not risk free. There are always concerns about putting people under general anesthesia. Things could happen, I suppose, which is why marrow donation appointments included a periodic review of my age, weight, blood pressure, blood iron levels, blood sugar levels before going to the hospital.

Being in the hospital as a well person is unusual. It's kind of like being in a mediocre hotel with no privacy and you want to wander the hallways because there is nothing you have to do except be ready for that one particular appointment first thing in the morning.

After the procedure the doctor in charge of the harvest came to my room, pleased to see me getting through recovery quickly. My sister walked me around the halls of the hospital before I was discharged. At some point that afternoon, the nurses told me that the marrow had been sent out and was now on its way to the recipient at Cleveland Clinic.

During my stay at the hospital I visited Chuck, one of my brother, Mike's, friends from our old neighborhood, someone I had been around since I was 5. He was diagnosed with his second bout of cancer in 2 years: the first was testicular; this second time the doctors found a brain tumor. When I saw him, his head was bandaged and he seemed slightly loopy. I was suddenly conscious that we had rarely talked one-on-one before.

As a kid, Chuck was powerfully built, though not tall. He was a bit of a bully, played football all through his teens. As an adult he became a burly bus mechanic with a distinctive laugh. As I talked with him, I thought about how young he was, 35 at the time. There were serious cancers among young people from that neighborhood.

At my house that afternoon, I napped and slept late the next morning. Before I met friends for the holiday weekend (careful to avoid vigorous physical activity, any lifting), I had to present myself to my mother. I thought that once I showed her I was okay, she would be somewhat mollified in her concerns.

"I don't think you realize how much stress you put on me, being angry with me about this."

"What do you want me to say, that I'm okay with this?"

"Well, yes…"

I didn't understand at the time that my mother had a particular need for attention and drama, to spin every situation to make herself the center of it while assuring us that she was easy to please. All of her children have lived away from her at some portions of our lives. She has viewed this not as an example of our professional or personal successes but as an inconvenience to her.

When I have lived nearby, I've been bombarded with questions about my siblings my mother doesn't want to ask them about directly, which makes her seem incurious about our lives. Instead, she talks about all her children behind their backs, like the neighborhood gossip.

"Is your sister planning to be here all weekend?"

"I don't know – did you ask her?"

She finds some behaviors risky in a way I find perplexing.

I was 16 sitting with her in the station wagon while we waited for my brother, Dennis, to buy a Bob Dylan concert ticket at the War Memorial box office. I saw a bearded man walk down the sidewalk, wearing a navy sport jacket and carrying a small bunch of folios, sheet music I would later realize. I knew immediately that it was Michael McDonald of The Doobie Brothers, as they were playing there that night. I was incredibly excited because I'd had a crush on him for a while. I told my mother who it was as I tore part of a shopping bag (the only paper I could find) to use to get his autograph. My mother insisted it was not him.

"Don't embarrass yourself."

I got out of the car realizing it was too humid for denim overalls, wondered about the shiny blouse underneath. I caught up with him and apologized for the scrap of paper.

He was lovely.

"How did you know who I am?"

"Well, I knew you were playing here tonight, so I figured..."

He smiled, signed the autograph and went on his way.

I really think my mother was disappointed that it was him. She didn't ask me a single question. I had not intended to see the show that night because I was trying to put myself on a budget. Besides, I'd seen The Doobie Brothers twice before. I changed my mind, went in and got my own ticket as my brother walked out.

Now in my parents' living room I was offering up information about how I was faring after the procedure and what I was learning about the bone marrow recipient. My father was genuinely happy to see me up and about.

"Do you have to see the doctor again?"

While my father talked, my mother went to the kitchen.

"No, but I should be getting an update about the recipient soon."

"Oh, that's nice."

**8**

# TRAVELING AND UNRAVELING

## JACQUELINE SCHMITT

Family lore is not often fact-checked. You trust the source—tales oft told after dinner, what you as a child overheard in another room or while dozing off as you were rocked to sleep. These stories feel true and real when you hear them, but they also feel distant. After all, they come from another country, from the past. These stories are connected to us in the present by the merest whisps and whispers. They are elusive and almost foreign.

"We have an ancestor who came from Southampton!" my mother used to say, joking about the riches in store if we ever laid claim to that old plot of family land where some celebrity has by now built a beach house.

This Southampton relative was my mother's grandfather's grandmother, and that's where we began when my son came home with an assignment from junior high school social studies to research his family tree.

"Henry Axtell, born 1798, Morristown, New Jersey," we found. "Nancy Haines, born 1795, Southampton, New York. Married 1828 in Morristown." How did she get from Long Island to New Jersey, we wondered? These two 30-somethings were unusually old for a first marriage in early America. How did they come to travel far from settled New Jersey to carve a farm out of the woods in Nelson, Madison County, New York? The town where my mother was born in 1926? And 30 miles from where we were living when my son was in junior high?

Early in their marriage, genealogical records tell us, Henry and Nancy lived not far from Morristown—only a few miles east in the town of Orange, New Jersey. Nancy bore three children in Orange; one died in infancy. By 1835, records say, the family lived in Nelson, New York. That was when and where their daughter Frances, was born: Frances, who in 1867 married James, and gave birth to Henry in 1870, Henry, my mother's grandfather. These stark facts at first glance revealed rich details, but really we know very little.

As I looked at this record of migration from New Jersey to upstate New York, I tried to place it within my own junior-high-school-social-studies understanding of how the west was won—at least the west of New York State as it was settled after the Revolutionary War. My assumptions were vague. I guessed that our forebears were among those Yankees who found farming too hard in New England and who moved west once the frontier was open.

Junior high school social studies offered me a benign view of those early years of Manifest Destiny. "The land was ours before we were the land's," wrote the poet Robert Frost[1]. I imagined those New England Yankees, standing on the dock in Albany, loading their household goods into boats for a leisurely journey west on the Erie Canal to lay claim to what was rightfully theirs.

My son may have been doing a school assignment, but I realized I was the one on the journey of discovery. I found facts, yes, but

---

1. Robert Frost, "The Gift Outright" https://www.poetryfoundation.org/poems/53013/the-gift-outright

they only raised more questions. First: the migration from New Jersey—not New England. How did a couple with two infants travel 200 miles over steep hills and river valleys? This territory is well known to me now but I speed over interstate highways, or choose to linger on picturesque two-lane roads. The New York State where my ancestors moved in 1835 is barely imaginable to me; it's as much a foreign country as some place on the other side of the globe.

Second: the land in Nelson. How did Henry and Nancy know that they could buy some land to farm and build a home? Who sold them this far away land? Did they know if the terrain was hilly and rocky? Was it fertile or was it a swamp? Those answers were shrouded in whisps and whispers. I began to think back to my own 7th-grade social studies class at LaFayette Central School, a mere 20 miles from that original farmstead in Nelson.

The Town of LaFayette took its name from the Marquis de Lafayette, Revolutionary War hero who made a victory lap across the Empire State in 1825. When my family moved to LaFayette in 1965, it was still largely farms and woodlots with a scattering of small housing developments resembling suburbs. U.S. Route 20 crosses through the center of town, following the old Cherry Valley Turnpike, one of the earliest east-west highways across New York State. It still is a popular route for those who prefer a more leisurely drive across open countryside and quaint towns.

Many of the settlements along Route 20 are marked by elegant, Federal-style buildings and prosperous businesses. LaFayette, on the other hand, is far more workaday in character. A classic white-steepled church sits at the intersection of Route 20 and Route 11, but so do a couple of gas stations, a discount store, and a 1960s mini-mall shared by the post office and a bank.

Mrs. Bush, my 7th-grade social studies teacher, lived in a building that also stands at that corner. She told us it dated from the early 19th century when it was a coaching inn that provided a good place to stop along this well-traveled road. It's empty now and shows its age in layers of remodeling, but if you step back you can see the outlines of wide, welcoming verandas.

Every day Mrs. Bush sat behind her desk and talked to us about New York State history. We each had a black and white composition notebook, and she told us to write down every word she said. She told us about the industries of New York—leather, salt, shoes, electricity from the great Niagara turbine, Syracuse China and Oneida Silverplate, Smith-Corona typewriters and International Business Machines and Herkimer cheese. All of it went into our black and white composition notebooks.

We learned the Revolutionary War was fought and won in New York State. Oriskany, the bloodiest battle. Saratoga, the turning point. Victories that choked off the British invasion before it began. We learned that the State of New York paid its brave veterans in land—including the very land on which our school was built. The Town of LaFayette is at the center of the Military Tract, 1.75 million acres of "bounty land," as the state called it in in 1781, divided into lots of 600 acres each.

Mrs. Bush was proud to point out that LaFayette had our very own cemetery—the final resting place of those Revolutionary veterans who settled in our town, who carved farmland out of woods, who built homesteads, who raised children and families, and whose descendants now sat beside me in my 7th-grade social studies classroom.

Wow, I thought. Cool. Actual Revolutionary War soldiers.

Mrs. Bush suggested we could learn more about the settling of New York State by reading some novels: *Drums Along the Mohawk. Dark Trees to the Wind. In the Hands of the Senecas. The Last of the Mohicans*[2] . I remembered seeing some old movie versions of them on Saturday afternoon tv. The heroes were handsome white movie stars, American even before there was an America. The Indians were scantily clad and swarthy, marked in Hollywood terms as "noble savages." They inevitably went down to defeat.

*Drums Along the Mohawk*, we wrote in our notebooks. In our modern New York State history in 1965, we were told that the "Mohicans" were long gone.

There were other children sitting beside me in seventh grade, children whose families also lived on this land in the 18th century. These were children who lived surrounded by the Town of LaFayette but whose history was not told by the buoyant accounts Mrs. Bush dictated into our black and white composition notebooks. These children grew up on the Onondaga Nation. They had attended their own elementary school but came to LaFayette for junior high and high school. This building in which they now sat was on the very land where their people had thrived for 1000 years before the birth of our American republic. What they heard from Mrs. Bush was an upside-down version of the history they already knew.

It took me 50 years to learn the lessons Mrs. Bush was teaching us in 7th-grade social studies. The military tract, that enabled veterans and their wives and children and children's children to move to

---

2. *Dark Trees to the Wind* by Carl Carmer. *Drums Along the Mohawk* and *In the Hands of the Senecas* by Walter D. Edmonds. *The Last of the Mohicans* by James Fenimore Cooper.

LaFayette, was created as the spoils of war. During the Revolution, the Onondaga fought alongside the British, but after the Battle of Oriskany—that one Mrs. Bush told us was the war's bloodiest—the Onondaga walked away from the conflict. Too many warriors died; they went back to their own land, west of the treaty line, to wait it out.

Then George Washington took revenge. In 1779, he sent the Continental Army to finish off the Onondaga and any other of the Six Nations who had sided with the British.

"The immediate objects are the total destruction and devastation of their settlements, and the capture of as many prisoners of every age and sex as possible," Washington commanded the generals. "It will be essential to ruin their crops now in the ground and prevent their planting more."[3]

John Sullivan and James Clinton marched a couple thousand troops north from Pennsylvania; Goose Van Schaick led 500 men west from the Mohawk Valley to Onondaga. They moved from town to town, taking prisoners, killing families, destroying villages, crops, storehouses. Van Schaick described how in one settlement "consisting of about fifty houses, a large quantity of corn and beans were burnt, a number of fine horses and every other kind of stock we found were killed."[4]

Thousands of Haudenosaunee fled west to Niagara. The trauma of the massacres was compounded by the coming winter, an exceptionally harsh one. More deaths resulted from disease and starvation. Defeated and disheartened, Onondaga and Cayuga leaders negoti-

---

3. From George Washington to Major General John Sullivan, 31 May 1779 https://
/founders.archives.gov/documents/Washington/03-20-02-0661

4. https://www.nps.gov/articles/000/the-van-schaick-expedition-april-1779.htm

ated small parcels of land from the new American government at the end of the war. New Yorkers took their millions of acres, and people like my family began to move in.

I am still looking at genealogical records and maps and I still wonder about the facts I began to uncover with my son's 7th-grade social studies assignment. My own 7th-grade social studies classes were full of stories of triumph. Of self-reliance. Of the superiority of European settlers and the inevitable destruction of everything in our way.

I write this in 2025, another time when the virtues we hope are embedded in our American experiment of a multi-cultural, settled democracy seem fainter than the drumbeats of expansion and entitlement.

It's time to retire Robert Frost's idea of "The Gift Outright." We need other poets now, poets who see us for who we are as well as who we aspire to be.

"Recognize whose lands these are on which we stand."

That is Jo Harjo's advice from her poem *Conflict Resolution for Holy Beings*.[5] Harjo, United States Poet Laureate from 2019 to 2022, writes,

> Recognize whose land this is on which we stand.
> Ask the deer, turtle, and the crane.
> Make sure the spirits of these lands are respected and treated with good will.
> The land is a being who remembers everything.

---

5. https://www.poetryfoundation.org/poems/141847/conflict-resolution-for-holy
 -beings

It's time to retrace the steps my ancestors took 200 years ago to get to those lands. It's time to stand where they stood, to see what is left of what they saw. It's time to listen to the land itself, because from what it remembers we can hear the possibility that even we can build a new future with respect and good will.

**9**

# RASCAL FLATTS/TAYLOR SWIFT CONCERT, 2008

LEE B. SAVIDGE

"Hi Dad, It's Shari."

"Hi Shari, what's up?"

"A friend gave me five tickets for the Rascal Flatts concert at the New York State Fair this weekend. That's one more than I need. He said I could sell it at the gate, but I'd rather share it with you."

"That's very thoughtful of you, Shari, and wow! That's some friend! Would you like to tell me about him?"

"No, Dad. It's just someone at work bought the tickets for his family, but his father died of a sudden heart attack, so now they can't go. Would you like to go to the concert?"

"Oh, how terrible for them! I feel strange to be both sad and happy at the same time. Isn't it ironic how sadness for them is lucky for us?...I'd love to join you, Shari...but, are you sure there isn't someone else you'd rather invite?"

"No, I'm going with my friend Mary and I'm dragging along your granddaughters, Megan (Shari's daughter), and Felisha (Shari's sister Lisa's daughter). I'd like you to join us, if you wouldn't mind being the only guy with us females."

"It sounds appealing. I'm not familiar with Rascal Flatts, but I know how you love country music. So I assume they're a country band."

"Yeah, sort of, and the opening act is Taylor Swift!"

"Who?"

"Taylor Swift! Megan and I love her. We know the words to all her songs."

"I like all kinds of music, including country. I just have not yet developed a taste for harsh screaming rock, where they repeat the same word or phrase over and over."

"These bands aren't like that, Dad. Their songs are more like ballads. They're very popular."

"You know, Shari, I haven't been to a concert since Olivia Newton John appeared at the War Memorial. That seems like 100 years ago. I purchased the highest price tickets, but still ended up a long way from the stage."

"These seats are near the center of the grandstand, and near the front of the upper level. They are far back from the stage but should be a clear view. And they're under the roof in case it rains."

"I've seen on TV how today's concerts use giant projection screens to make sure even the last row in the back gets a good view. Thanks, Shari, I think it sounds like a wonderful event."

"That's great Dad. I have a lot of errands to run, so I'll bring the ticket to you on the way. You can use it to enter the Fair this weekend and join us at the Mohegan Sun Grandstand for the concert. It has a funny name. It's called the Bob That Head Tour."

"I'll look forward to it."

Shari arrived and gave me an envelope and a hug. I knew she wouldn't have time to stay.

I was aglow with anticipation as my green-handled opener unzipped the envelope. The note read, "Looking forward to seeing you. Love, Shari." She always dots the "i" in her name with a tiny circle or a tiny heart. This time it was a heart.

On August 31st, 2008, the day of the concert, I parked at Fairmount shopping plaza and caught the shuttle to the New York State Fair. The shuttle was easier than parking at the fairgrounds, especially on crowded concert nights.

As the bus rambled along, I pulled the ticket out of my pocket again just to make triply sure I still had it. The fair came into view and I could see the colorful flashing lights of the Ferris wheel at the midway towering above the tops of the many buildings. Loudspeakers were announcing various shows and events. Ushered by police controlling the traffic, the bus pulled onto the curved driveway in front of the main gate. First the hiss of air brakes and then the bus doors swung open. I lumbered down the steps and joined in one of several lines of people filing through the turnstiles. Concert ticket holders enter the fair no extra charge. I was grateful to avoid the long ticket lines.

My first stop is always the Dairy Building, to savor a glass or two of 25 cent chocolate milk, while I admire the butter sculpture. The sculptures are made with 800 pounds of butter and are mounted on a large rotating turntable so viewers can scan every detail. Over the years I've seen lots of butter scenes with adults and/or children enjoying an assortment of dairy products while participating in various recreational activities. I've also seen many versions of cows, even a sculpture of a cow on hind legs in a milk delivery van doorway with its front legs spread wide as if to hug the audience. This time the sculpture depicted a cow jumping over the moon.

I worked my way down the streets and aisles past the myriad of vendors hawking clothing, sunglasses, taffy, western style hats, lemonade, car polish, and you-name-it. The cooking smells of spicy sausage, peppers and onions, barbecue, popcorn, and pizza frittes permeated the air.

The closer I got to the grandstand, the tighter the crowd of wall-to-wall people. The mouthwatering smells of culinary treats were suddenly diminished by a scent of body odor. I turned and spotted the culprit, a sweaty, thick armed, heavily tattooed, pony-tailed, unshaven, beer-bellied guy. His chest hair poked from under the low neckline of his food stained sleeveless white T-shirt. A voluptuous blond tagged along with him despite the scent.

I wove my way through the crowd away from the unpleasant odor. In the middle of an intersection ahead a man held a sign in the air. He turned in a gradual circle so all in the vicinity could get a glimpse. It read, "Need 2 tickets, pay $100 each." For an instant I considered selling my $66 ticket and giving the 100 dollars to Shari. I knew she could put the money to good use. But I decided against subjecting my daughter and granddaughters to the surprise of some stranger taking my seat.

At Section 2, Row LL, I greeted my family members with smiles and hugs. My seat was to the right of a large steel column. I felt sorry for the people to my left who were behind the column. Then I saw there were two giant projection screens, one on each side of the stage, so all could have a good view. Looking down from the upper level, the sea of heads and shoulders below me rippled like water in the wind.

My teenage granddaughters stretched their arms out straight with cell phone cameras in hand. They took pictures of themselves sitting side-by-side as they leaned toward each other, almost cheek-to-cheek; the arms not holding cameras were on each other's shoulders.

The sun was setting, the pink and purple sky growing dim, but the stage gleamed bright. The positions for band members spanned the width of the stage with an assortment of guitars, drums, keyboard, piano and other instruments and equipment. Huge speakers and amps towered high on both sides of the stage. The backdrop was a billboard-sized picture of a cute young pale skinned, blond woman's face wearing bright red lipstick and a cowboy hat. Her full lips were closed, slightly smiling and slightly puckered, as though she wanted a kiss. Her expression exuded confidence and her large bright blue eyes stared right at me. Large letters across the top said, "Taylor Swift."

As band members began emerging from the shadows, taking positions behind music stands and strapping on instruments, the crowd roared. Even before Taylor Swift was introduced, the audience glistened with the glow of 17,000 cell phones and digital camera screens all held high. The announcement came from speakers everywhere, "Recording is forbidden." Yeah, right, I want to see them try to arrest 17,000 people.

The band started playing and Taylor Swift was introduced. With light from so many cell phone screens, I could see about 80% of the audience had long hair. Some longhaired men might have been among them, but the pitch of the roar proved the audience was mostly female. To my surprise, everyone jumped to their feet and remained standing.

Taylor Swift marched across the stage from right to left and back again to the music's beat, a slender young woman with her blond hair hanging down past her shoulders. She wore a short sleeve pale yellow dress with a modest neckline and hem below the knees. The hem puffed out, as though there might be a petticoat underneath. It sprung forward at the knee with each marching step Taylor took. Her slender legs were like soda straws extending to her matching yellow spikes. Imagine a blond Barbie with a microphone in her hand.

Taylor started singing with her smooth, sweet, somewhat sultry voice. I liked her blend of modern and traditional country music, even though the audience's singing along fuzzed the sound. I could not quite understand all the words. As the entire audience sang along, I briefly felt out of place. I was in the minority by age, by sex, and by not knowing the lingo. But I didn't want to be anywhere else at that moment. So I stood joyfully swaying to the music with my granddaughters by my side.

Taylor opened with *I'm Only Me When I'm With You*. The line, "I'm only up when you're not down," stuck with me. In the song *Change*, memorable lines included, "It's hard to fight when the fight ain't fair...But there's something in your eyes...Says we can beat this."

When Taylor Swift was done and Rascal Flatts was introduced, the audience roar was almost deafening. The lights illuminating Taylor's backdrop picture were turned off and a laser light show began. The name "Rascal Flatts" lit up in bright neon. The band was dressed in casual dark jeans and black leather vests.

Gary LeVox, the lead vocalist, took the spotlight behind the microphone. His short light-brown spiked style hair was gleaming in the bright light. He looked middle-aged, older than most of his audience, but handsome with a slightly stocky build. I was surprised his group was just a trio. His cousin, Jay DeMarcus, did bass guitar, keyboard, piano and vocals. And the lead guitarist, Joe Don Rooney, also did vocals.

They opened with the song *Still Feels Good*. The second song, *Life Is A Highway*, was the only song familiar to me. I joined the singing for a few lines. "Life is a highway...I wanna ride it all night long." They played 18 songs all together ending with *Bob That Head*, but again the audience's singing applied a murmured overtone to all the songs and I could hardly understand a word. I loved the upbeat country rock sound. And the multicolored laser light show was dramatic. I did not notice my feet hurt from all that standing until after the concert was over and the crowd started exiting the venue like endlessly long, slow moving centipedes. Shari asked me where I parked. When I told her Fairmount plaza, she insisted on driving me there.

"Shari, I'm not used to standing in one spot for 3 or 4 hours. Are all concerts like this today?"

"Standing is common, but they don't usually stand for the opening band too. Did you like the concert, Dad?"

"Yes, except for sore feet, I loved it!"

On January 9th, 2016, I felt a sense of loss as I watched the implosion. The massive Mohegan Sun Grandstand collapsed to the ground in seconds. A new concert venue at the Onondaga Lake shore, across the street from the New York State Fairgrounds, would relieve the former congestion of wall-to-wall people on concert nights, but I had a strong twinge of nostalgia for my August 2008 experience with my daughter and granddaughters.

NF0831
EVENT CODE
$ 66.50
8.30
SECTION/AISLE
GSTD 2
MC    25X
ROW    SEAT
LL    75
ZWS756A
12JUN08
GSTD 2  LL  75        AFULL
SECTION/AISLE    ROW/BOX    SEAT        ADMISSION
GRANDSTAND RIGHT         66.50
BOB THAT HEAD TOUR 2008
RASCAL FLATTS
WITH GUEST TAYLOR SWIFT
NEW YORK STATE FAIR
MOHEGAN SUN GRANDSTAND
SUN, AUG 31 2008 7:30PM

# 10

## THE CAPUCHIN CRYPT

### KATHY ROTHENBERG

"If you're up to it, take a look," Gary said, placing the travel guide on the kitchen table.

I drank my tea and thumbed through the pages my husband had marked up with notes and highlights while he continued talking.

"I just booked our last hotel. The owner sent me a confirmation and said the view from our room is *magnifico*."

I closed the travel guide and sighed.

"Thirty days for thirty years," he said, referring to the amount of time we would be staying in Italy to celebrate our upcoming wedding anniversary.

"Yeah, sounds great, but let's talk about it another time."

He gave me a concerned look that had become too familiar.

It was late winter, and I was still in the throes of chemotherapy. Getting out of bed every morning was a challenge; on a good day, a walk around the block was a major accomplishment; traipsing around Italy for a month was unfathomable.

I had once shared his enthusiasm, was even the one who suggested the trip while we sat in Adirondack chairs by a mountain lake the previous summer.

"The first thing I want to do when we retire is go to Italy."

"I'm in," he replied, already thinking of the research he would do. Planning trips was his favorite hobby.

That was before my diagnosis of ovarian cancer, when things were normal—a time when the fear of dying didn't keep me awake at night.

My official retirement from teaching followed several months of sick leave and coincided with the end of my chemo treatments in the spring. That summer, I joined the Livestrong program at the YMCA. Alongside other survivors, I began a regimen of exercise to get back in shape. In addition to strength-building classes and yoga, I walked every day. As fall approached, I was doing 4-mile stretches without getting winded. My eagerness to travel returned, but I still didn't want to read the guidebooks Gary had strategically left around the house.

"Just surprise me," I said.

On a crisp September day, two days before my 62nd birthday, we boarded a plane to Italy. Our first stop was Lake Como, nestled in the foothills of the Alps. We raised our wineglasses in a silent toast, letting our thoughts capture the many things we had to celebrate, as we gazed at the fairytale-like setting. Limestone streaking the mountains created an illusion of snow-covered trails in the late day sun while glints of light danced on the surface of the aqua blue water. The magic of that moment stayed with us throughout the days that followed.

Towards the end of our trip, we joined the throngs of tourists at the Vatican and Coliseum. On our last day in Rome, a pleasant exhaustion had set in.

"Today, let's go somewhere off the beaten path," I said.

"Okay, do you remember when I mentioned the Capuchin Crypt while I was planning the trip?"

"Um . . . not really."

"I came across a brief write-up on it. It isn't frequented by tourists like many of the places we've been, but it sounds unique. Want to check it out?"

"Sure," I said, wondering what would be so special about a crypt. We had seen several of them in the bowels of cathedrals where saints or bishops were often buried.

Gary pulled up the maps of Rome he had downloaded on his cell phone, and we set out from our hotel on foot. When we reached the Church of Santa Maria della Concezione, the GPS alerted us, *you have arrived at your destination.*

The church was nondescript from the outside and much smaller than the large, ornate cathedrals we had visited. Part of the first floor had been converted into a museum depicting the history of the Capuchins, an order of Friars founded in 1209. We read the placards in the display cases and learned that the monks were the original followers of St. Francis of Assisi. They lived an austere life, free of worldly possessions, and dedicated their lives to prayer and meditation.

When the next tour of the crypt was announced, we joined a small group of people waiting to enter. Our guide asked us to remain silent as we descended the stairs leading into the dank hallways of the cavern below. Flickering candles cast eerie shadows as we made our way to the first of six chambers. It was named the Crypt of the Resurrection and contained a huge painting of Jesus raising Lazarus from the dead. On closer inspection of the frame surrounding the painting, I discovered it was comprised of human bones.

The second room was a chapel used to celebrate Mass. It contained a simple wooden altar with a cross above it. As our group shuffled into the next chamber, the Crypt of Skulls, I heard a gasp from the front of the line. Thousands of human skulls mounted tightly together covered the surrounding walls of the crypt. A sea of hollowed-out faces stared at us, daring us to stare back, while two mummified bodies in hooded cloaks stood watch.

Our guide directed us back into the hallway and spoke in a hushed tone. "The bones of 4,000 Capuchin Friars are buried in these chambers. When the monks arrived at this church in 1631, possibly fleeing persecution in France, they brought 300 cartloads of deceased friars from their former monastery with them. As more monks died during the lifetime of the crypt, the bodies that had been there the longest were exhumed to make room for the newly deceased. Bodies took about 30 years to decompose in the soil. When the monks reclaimed the bones, they used them to make the decorative artwork you will see next."

*Decorative artwork?*

Gary leaned in close and filled my ear with a low, ghoulish laugh. I gave him a stern look and put my finger to my lips. Then I checked the location of the closest exit.

The next three chambers bore the following names: Crypt of Pelvises, Crypt of Leg Bones, and Crypt of Three Skeletons. Heart shapes made from hipbones, and flowers created from ribs and vertebrae, formed intricate mosaic patterns adorning the walls and ceilings. Baroque-style chandeliers, crafted from a mix of skeletal remains, hung from the ceiling; a gigantic clock made of leg and foot bones filled one wall. The monks had painstakingly crafted these artful masterpieces to honor their dead. Entombed in these walls of death was a reverence for life.

The last crypt was the only one containing entire skeletons. A chilling sign written in multiple languages contained the following quote: "*What you are now we used to be; what we are now, you will be.*"

I took a deep breath and let the words sink in. *No one is spared*, I thought. *I am not alone.*

"Well, that was creepy," Gary said, once we were outside.

"I don't know, I found it kind of peaceful."

He stared at me, that look of concern returning.

"Don't worry, I plan to be around a long time before I become a wall ornament. But when the time comes, I'm thinking a butterfly might be nice."

We both laughed as he reached for my hand, and we walked back to our hotel to ready ourselves for the journey home.

# 11

## OUR WINTER OF SCALLOPED POTATOES

### GEORGIA A. POPOFF

From the kitchen of our second-floor flat, my roommates and I could see the hills of the University neighborhood stretching into the eastern horizon. At night, the hills sparkled with streetlights and the glow from countless windows.

Connor, Maureen, and I scraped our $200 rent together somehow every month. This was the mid-70s and we were young, fairly unencumbered. I waited tables until I got my "big break" into a "real job" at the AAA, first in hotel/motel reservations during warmer seasons, and winter duty was, of course, emergency road service. Connor was doing aluminum siding, loading all of his equipment in and on top of his tiny blue Toyota Corolla. The break and ladders stretched well beyond both front and rear bumpers, a humorous sight. Maureen was working with Connor at times, and then she got a job as an assistant to a portrait photographer. All three of us were broke but unrelenting in having a good time.

We needed a refrigerator to replace the broken one that our shady landlord would not. Somehow, we came upon a funky old 1950s refrigerator. In spite of the heft of the appliance's thick glass packing, Connor and Maureen's mother's boyfriend, Dennis, made it up the back stairs a step at a time. Connor thought Dennis was going to have a heart attack right in the stairwell. But they persevered and we then had a functional fridge! Not only functional but Fab Fifties wonderful. It purred and did its job.

On a whim, we committed to eating all of our meals with chopsticks, except for pancakes and pizza. Somehow, pancakes lose their integrity with chopsticks. And, well, pizza is self-explanatory. We decided on this plan based on a combination of the fact that Connor was stationed in Japan and Okinawa when he was in the service, and my mom taught me how to use chopsticks when I was 10. Anyway, it seemed like a civilized idea, even sophisticated. We taught most of our friends how to negotiate meals without forks. We always set the table for guests with both a set of chopsticks and the standard flatware. We offered the instruction and encouraged our friends to try chopsticks first and then, as frustration set in, we let them off the hook while we continued with our own deft dining skills.

Maureen's mother, Rose, sometimes showed up with bags of groceries. Rice and beans were one staple in the face of our financial limits, and we relied on a vast bounty of potatoes, finding many ways to make them satisfying. One frigid early winter night, Maureen sliced potatoes and layered them with dabs of butter, sprinkles of salt and pepper, a bit of flour, and delicate onion rings in our big yellow Pyrex mixing bowl, then added milk. As the casserole baked, the alchemy filled the kitchen with the aroma of our meal that would not only feed us that night but for several to come. They were crispy on the top and creamy with the milk and starch that cooked together into a rib-sticking goo.

Rose's friend, Dennis, managed an all-night diner not far from where we lived. He knew that we were all scraping even though we all worked. Dennis gave us a big box of frozen sausage patties to help us out. He gave us other foodstuffs, too, but that stash of disks of a gray-brown meat substance is a vivid memory. Oh boy…time to get creative with the facsimile of protein. Who would ever look a gift sausage in the mouth? At the time, fake meat seemed better than no meat and the spices were welcomed.

Maureen knew just what to do…a topper to the scalloped potatoes! That added a twist to the winter staple, a new flavor, and hey, we thought maybe we might benefit nutritionally as well. Since Maureen and I had both grown up in homes where money was often tight, we developed a skill for cooking great meals out of next to nothing, starting when Maureen and I lived together the first time several years before in another second-floor flat in a different neighborhood while attending the local community college.

My mom had been great at turning out a full menu from scant staples. She was also very adept at convincing us, as kids, that pancakes or cereal for dinner was a special treat rather than the sad truth that Daddy only got paid biweekly and sometimes all she had was cereal, flour, a couple of eggs, some milk, and a big bottle of Log Cabin. We didn't care…sugar-based dinner. Yahoo…

So I came to inventive meal planning easily. To this day, I have a cupboard filled with beans of all sorts, odd canned goods that I stash, pastas, a freezer of soup stock and such from when I cook other meals, an abundance to draw upon. It would take me at least a month of no shopping to see the back of the shelves and I frequently have to rearrange everything just to retrieve a can of tomato paste or tuna.

Anyway, my roommates and I were never so broke that we could not entertain. We have always loved dinners with friends and in the years that we shared a home, there were countless wonderful meals. That kitchen on Teall Avenue was huge and we could easily fit eight around our table. It had a warm, homey sense with the bright yellow paint, the country-striped wallpaper, white trim, all of which we had added to the room when we moved in. Connor used scrap wood from a job to make a butcher-block style counter under the double windows facing south, polyurethaned to a high gloss. Our aforementioned refrigerator partnered with an equally funky old stove. We laughed a great deal there. Friends were always in the house, stopping by to hang out, or coming in from out of town for a few days. It was a central location and we loved all of it.

When the weather grew warm, we spent a lot of time on our small porch nestled into the boughs of the tree in front of our house. Teall Avenue is a major thoroughfare so there was always traffic. Across the street there was an old firehouse converted to a flower shop on one corner and on the other, a pizza shop and corner store. There was an ever-present source of entertainment watching the street action. Connor would sometimes practice his saxophone out on the porch and the whole neighborhood rang with his notes. When the leaves filled in, it was quite private and we sat on the porch nearly invisible, laughing at the world below.

The weeks we got paid, meals were better. Pasta, burgers, pork chops, lots of salad and veggies. Somehow we also managed afford-able wine and beer. Sometimes our guests provided the beverages, a fair exchange. There was rarely a quiet weekend evening and always lots of laughter. We weren't overly serious. We were still in our 20s, we still had few concerns beyond the immediate, and we worked at enjoying ourselves, sometimes as a way to forget the difficulties that had already clouded our individual lives. I don't think I have ever lived so much in the moment as I did the 3 years that Maureen, Connor, and I were roommates. Maybe it was the times. Maybe it was all those scalloped potatoes.

# 12

## THE SNOWY HILLS BEYOND

AARON M. PERRINE

*And further: the stages that mark the wayfarers' journey from
their mortal abode to the heavenly homeland are said to be
seven. Some have referred to them as seven valleys, and others,
as seven cities. And it is said that until the wayfarer taketh
leave of self and traverseth these stages, he shall never attain the
ocean of nearness and reunion nor taste of the matchless wine.*
*"The Seven Valleys" by Bahá'u'lláh*
*from The Call of the Divine Beloved*

The defining geographic feature of the "Crown City" of New York where I grew up is the "crown" in the center of the city of Cortland—I always heard it called Court House Hill—the center of seven valleys carved by glaciers during the last ice age. I used to ride along with my mother to pay the electric bill at the local office of the utility on that hill. I remember being puzzled at why the locals called it Court House Hill, as the courthouse was at the bottom of it. Only later did I learn that the first courthouse used to be on the side of that hill. The one I knew is the third and still stands.

Built in 1813, the first courthouse served until 1836. Books of local lore tell stories of lawyers and litigants climbing the hill in winter to the first courthouse to conduct the legal business of early Cortland County.

My childhood home was also on a hill, not the crown but one between two of the seven valleys. The one that leads to Groton lies to the south, and the one that leads to Locke to the north. The latter has a name—Kinney Gulf—presumably named for an early settler. Our house was close to halfway up the hill; I can recall a few instances of my school bus having a lot of difficulty restarting the climb in the winter after stopping to pick up my brother and me from the end of our relatively steep driveway. There was a repeat of this problem on my kindergarten bus route; the bus stopped on another hill, again approximately halfway up, higher than the one I lived on, to pick up a girl I didn't know well who later died too young of cancer. Just past her house the road became a seasonal limited use highway—a term of art in New York for a road that is not paved and receives no snow clearing. I can't remember what the bus driver did after the girl got on the bus, although I remember his name. We must have simply turned around.

That hill was between Kinney Gulf and a third valley, the one that leads north from the Village of Homer to Preble and beyond. This valley is, by my eye, the broadest around my hometown: farms; two state highways and one interstate; gravel mining, historically; and one of the railroads that once served Cortland, and the only one that still does, are all there. Also, the homes of many of my childhood friends were in this valley; some still live there. Two dear friends and their children keep bees on the hillside that separates this valley from the next one to the east.

A friend of my brother's once told us the story of how a radio transmission tower was built on this hill in the 1950s. The tower was built in the winter, with the pieces hauled by a local farmer to the ridge at the top in a horse-drawn sleigh. I've tried, and partially succeeded, to impress upon my son how unusual this was as late as it was done.

This fourth valley leads northeast to the village of Truxton and beyond. Another dear friend and I chose our route out of this valley very poorly one afternoon and found ourselves on one of those limited use highways, trying to drive over the hill and into the valley to the village of Homer. His carefully repaired Volkswagen Beetle, which had an engine fire, made it through the ruts and washouts from the rain and snow runoff. This journey was not in the winter, of course; it was late summer, just before school, and the road was dry.

The fifth valley leads south to Blodgett Mills; yet another good friend lived on a farm on the hill between the this valley and the one that leads to Truxton. The sixth valley, to Virgil and the seventh, to Dryden. Part of the hill between those last two valleys is in a city park, known for hard-packed snow from intensive sledding by local children throughout the winter. The kind of snow where you could actually use a runner sled to achieve some real speed. My brother had one then and still has it.

If geography has so much to do with how we live and who we are, I am tempted to say that Cortland County has more power to shape us than other places, but that sort of hometown boosterism should be suspect; close the book if someone writes "character forged by the hills and valleys and the falling snow," or something similar.

I have indulged in something that you could call anti-boosterism, though, across both time and place. Courthouses on hills with no doubt well-dressed folks trudging through snow-banks to get to them. Seasonal limited use highways that are rough in spring, summer, and fall and useless in winter, except as places for high school students to drink and get high away from observation.

Even the sledding, one of the glories of upstate New York childhood, could be both cheered and condemned. Cortland's Beaudry Park, where my brother and I could achieve such tremendous speed, banned sledding from time to time. It was banned in Syracuse, my home now, officially in 1933, but the police unofficially chased kids away from popular hills at least as long ago as 1908, following a child's death when he was struck by a streetcar. The ban was ignored on Libe Slope at Cornell University in Ithaca; the old trees menacing as the students slide on purloined dining hall trays.

And the snow, always the snow. The storms that roar northeast. Alternatively, the warm water picked up and into the air from Lake Ontario dropped, frozen, without ceremony and relentlessly, all winter. My wife and her family, native Buffalonians, would get some relief when shallow Lake Erie would freeze; Lake Ontario's depth keeps the lake effect machine, as the weather forecaster's cliché goes, running all winter long most years.

I have been lucky in my life to travel—it is a true love of my wife's. In search of some of her family history, we were able go to Belgium and Luxembourg to explore the Wallonian village Messancy, not much larger than the city where I grew up. We took the train from Brussesls. It was striking to see the hills from the rail car we rode in. When we dropped off the step and onto the platform it seemed so very familiar. Maybe I was primed to feel it; my father, a reluctant traveler who did so primarily for work, once told me that the place that felt most familiar to him was the hills outside of Seoul, South Korea.

I feel as though I can know a little of someone who grew up in Wallonia or Korea—you understand why at least four different languages were and are spoken along the relatively short journey from Brussels to Luxembourg City. It was so difficult to share culture when there are hills and snow keeping you away from the folks who live in the next valley. I think of the Haudenosaunee and the difficulty and sacrifice of forming a confederation across the upstate New York geography—the lakes and hills. But also there is the difficulty of forming communal government across the language barriers, across the cultural differences, across divides created not only by the weight of glaciers, but by the weight of historical inertia.

I think of Freud's narcissism of small differences—I went to Homer Central Schools, in that village, and those who lived around Truxton went to school there until sixth grade, when they joined us. Did we ever tease them! Another lifelong friend raised there and went to school there. We acted as though we were the sophisticates, educated one valley over. Homer was Manhattan, Montreal, London, Lagos, Tehran, Rio—urbane.

The excerpt from "The Seven Valleys" at the beginning of this was a happy research coincidence; I didn't know of it before I looked for the phrase "seven valleys" to see what I could find on various websites. Curiosity led me to one of the tenets of the Báha'í faith: the emphasis on the unity of all people and how we are so very diverse. That is not so easy to put into practice, even if the only consideration is not teasing someone about where they went to school.

I remember learning about two years after sixth grade how human nature always interferes with human plans for utopia. I was 14 when the Berlin Wall was torn down, so I am certain that lesson was focused on the ultimate unworkability of Communist economies.

Humans have wants, want choices to fulfill those wants, and moreover those wants are diverse.

But what shape, what geography, is that utopia? There is a powerful tendency within us to perceive that which is familiar as being not just familiar, but right. Call it a variation on the naturalist fallacy. Call out Plato for stating the only just government is ruled by a philosopher-king, which is convenient when you are a philosopher. Call me out for not realizing that the government that was supposed to come into being after the fall of Soviet Communism—the government at the end of history, Francis Fukuyama called it—looked very much like our government at that moment. I didn't realize at the time there was something about that coincidence that should have been looked into more deeply.

But forgive me, I was only 14. We were all young and perhaps all naive once, we are all from somewhere. Some from many places, me from essentially only one, and I suppose none of us can help search for meaning from that which we are most familiar. That familiarity is a tremendously important part of who we are while also being a nearly intractable limitation to our thought at the same time. I wouldn't trade my youth for anything, because I love the stories of snow, sleds, sleighs, hills, and valleys. I also love the friends I acquired among it all.

But I came to admire other stories. My wife's stories of internationalism, inspired by the founding of the European Union. The possibility of travel as a way to overcome provincialism, that possibility made reality with a lot of help from her. The possibility of metaphorical language and translation to see at least a bit of what someone like Bahá'u'lláh had to say about unity and yes, utopia, for all of its practical impossibility. If you were born in the confluence of seven valleys, it would be a mistake to never climb the highest hill, even through the snow in winter, to try to glimpse that which lies beyond where you began.

# 13

## SOLO ADVENTURE IN CHINA

MARY J. NOWYJ

There's no place like home, there's no place like home," exclaimed Dorothy in the "Wizard Of Oz," written by Frank Baum. Originally, Dorothy had been thinking about a different life growing up in rural Kansas until a tornado came and tossed her into an unusual new world, unfamiliar to her. Sometimes, our own personal experiences can leave us wishing we could return to more familiar ground.

My personal adventure experiences had thrust me into various travel situations where I was thrilled to explore new countries to learn, meet people, and explore the geography. Yet after a while, I wanted to return home to more comfortable terrain and familiarity. Perhaps it was homesickness, similar to what I felt as a child when I visited grandparents in other cities. Perhaps I was only frightened by my new surroundings. Either way, I wanted to go home.

As an adult, I had one traveling experience that I pursued after finishing my graduate degree. I had the opportunity to learn the Chinese language and history of the culture. Two years later, Professor Chen invited me to teach in China for a short period in 1990, a year after the Tiananmen Square student protests in Beijing.

"You be pioneer for this new college in Zhengzhou, Henan Province," he said. "There will be other professors who will join you."

My first thought was affirmative. My second thought was that's too far away from home for me. Yet, mentally, I was craving a huge change in my life. My friend Rita called it a mid-life crisis.

At age 40, I wanted some new experiences before I got too old to try anything out of the ordinary and surely teaching in China would be very challenging. My husband was involved with his business and my children were in college working on their lives. So, after carefully investigating the particulars of time, getting proper documentation, and talking to previous teachers from my area who taught there, I made the commitment to spend a few months traveling solo.

It was late winter and I went to a park to cross-country ski, where I met a visiting scholar from China. I mentioned my new adventure. Her name was Chen Hong. We discussed when I would be going and she would help me when I arrived in Beijing. She was going home that summer.

"Traveling alone as a single woman in China is challenging," Chen said. "I live in Beijing, so, I can show you around the city."

"Oh, thank you so much," I replied.

Before Chen left to go home, we discussed my plans again more thoroughly. I felt so much more adventurous that day. I also had contacted Li Wei, my former Chinese language professor who gave me her address in Beijing.

As fall and the time for my trip approached, I became more enthusiastic. I had my passport, proper papers, shots, tickets, all set. What I wasn't prepared for was the phone call from Professor Wang.

"Are you all set for your trip? You will be met at the airport with a guide who will take care of your affairs," he said.

"I am looking forward to meeting all the other teachers."

Professor Wang responded with, "Oh, there are no other teachers! You are the only one invited, and you will be a pioneer."

That's when I got concerned. Since I was leaving the next morning, I wasn't sure what to do. I was at a loss for words. I felt conflicted. Then I thought, If this doesn't work out, I will be home on the next plane.

My husband, Steve, and my oldest daughter brought me to the airport. Suddenly, my husband reached into his coat pocket and gave me a letter and a huge hug.

Steve said, "I know this will be a great learning lesson for you. I will be waiting for your return home."

We all hugged tightly and then I entered the gate for my plane with a bit of trepidation knowing I was facing an adventure alone. Yet, I had faith that all would work out for the best. I believed in divine providence.

The flight took 22 hours with only one transfer. I had a seat on a huge, luxurious airline where I could sleep in comfort. When I finally arrived at the gate and met my guide, Zhang, I was also greeted by Chen Hong, the scholar I met in Syracuse. When she returned back to her home in China, she had contacted college staff to ask if she could attend my welcome greeting. I felt comforted with such concern for me.

Driving through Beijing to the Friendship Hotel was stimulating. I saw large signs in Chinese, beautiful colorful trees, and many people walking with large bags, possibly filled with groceries. I also saw many children on playgrounds. Although the sky was a bit grey, I enjoyed the atmosphere. After settling in at the hotel, which was modern, I called my husband to let him know I safely arrived. We talked for quite a while. I promised to call him daily.

Early the next day I had a visit from Chen Hong and her daughter. She shared with me that I should be very careful perhaps, since my daily activities were being monitored. She gave me her personal information should I need assistance. Again, I felt more at ease and thanked her.

After Chen left, I decided to walk around the city to view the area. The streets were crowded with people walking and riding bicycles. I saw children playing in gated schoolyards. Finally, I decided to take a taxi to visit my Chinese teacher, Li Wei, who had come back to Beijing. Her living conditions were much smaller than the one she had in Syracuse. We were so happy to see each other. She also cautioned me to stay close to the hotel area when I returned for the day.

After a few days of exploring the city area, Zhang said, "It is time for us to leave for the University. We need to reach the train station in time for boarding."

When we arrived, so many people were sitting on the platform with their bags.

"It's very crowded," I exclaimed.

Zhang acknowledged, "Yes, this is the major form of transportation, but you will have a cabin with three other people, so you can sleep. I will have to sit up front with others, but I will be back for you in the morning." I felt reassured. We walked down the aisle to my cabin.

Inside, there were four bunks, two up, two down. The three other passengers were Chinese men. I felt uncomfortable and motioned that I would like an upper bunk. They nodded their heads. We communicated a little in Chinese. Later that evening, while trying to sleep, I heard soft music in the cabin. I wondered, what am I doing here?

The next morning, Zhang came to get me for breakfast. We went to the dining car for breakfast and enjoyed a nice conversation. Seeing Zhang was relaxing. I felt safe.

"I hope your evening went well," he said. "We will be arriving soon at the train station, and a taxi will take us to the University. There will be a tour of the campus, also." I responded with much enthusiasm even after a sleepless night.

After getting my luggage off the train, I was a bit confused by my surroundings. Everyone was in a hurry, and I felt anxious watching the scurrying. Suddenly, Zhang pulled me aside and we entered a car. We drove for about 30 minutes through farmland until we reached a large iron gate with a sign announcing in Chinese, YELLOW RIVER UNIVERSITY. The campus was on 1,200 acres of farmland. Suddenly, I felt nervous being so far away from home. I was very tired and dehydrated.

I learned I could only consume boiled water, which had to cool down before drinking, so, I had to be careful. After finding my accommodations in an old large building, I settled in for the evening.

In the early morning, I walked down a wooded dirt path to the dining hall where I had breakfast with other Chinese residents, as well as Zhang. After being introduced, I was given a tour of the campus with various orders to not meet with students at their living quarters. I had a few leather couches outside my bedroom to meet with them at certain times if needed. That's when I started to feel uneasy. I did get to see other buildings and took some photos of the area as the tour progressed. But, it was the next day when I had time alone to discover the grounds.

As I walked around the deep woods, I spotted a few habitats that may have been small homes, except there were iron bars across the open area close to the ground. I saw people peering out at me. Not wanting to bother them I continued on my walk. Then, I viewed large old farm buildings with silos. A man on a bicycle was in the road, just observing me. As I walked more, I saw various headstones scattered around a shallow area. It was a small, unkept cemetery with a lot of brown grass.

I felt chilled at the site. I began to get very uncomfortable. That was the beginning of my homesickness. I felt insecure. I wondered why this was in the compound.

Although I never saw him during the day, there was a security guard every night just below my room. He paced around as if he were looking for someone. My mind began to question a number of conditions. I was alone all the time. There was no one to talk to about when the students would arrive, or any written schedule for engagements. I became more concerned. I wanted to call home, but was not given permission until further notice. I felt like a prisoner. I just wanted to go home. I had a contract, yet I knew this was not a good place for me mentally or physically.

I decided to talk with Zhang and explain the situation as carefully as I could, apologizing for the inconvenience I caused. He understood and we went to talk with the president of the university.

At first, he would not let me go, but then I said, "You can detain me here, but I will not speak."

Zhang went back once more and returned saying, "He will let you go, but we must hurry before he changes his mind. Let's go and get your belongings and to the airport to get a ticket to Hong Kong."

When we arrived at the airport, a young American man who had taught at the University before was coming our way. Zhang introduced me as a new teacher, but she has to leave.

The man said, "It is best that you leave now, since it is not safe for you here in China."

We said our goodbyes, and after I got my ticket, Zhang wished me a safe return. Overwhelmed with all my documents and boarding pass, I became confused. I saw an older Caucasian man sitting on a bench, so I approached him. He spoke English and was able to help me with the protocol for boarding. I felt like I had divine providence.

"Thank you so much," I said.

After everyone was boarded on the plane, I looked over to see the same man sitting across from me. We began to talk about what my purpose was in Zhengzhou. When I mentioned the university, he said, laughing, "That's no college, it is a prison."

Even though I did not take him seriously, I realized I felt like a prisoner at times. Earlier, he told me he had been in Zhengzhou on business many times, so, maybe he knew more.

When we arrived in Hong Kong, I had no idea where I would go next. The man asked, "Would you like to ride in the taxi to the city with me?"

"Of course, that would be nice," I responded.

After riding for about 20 minutes and sharing information about family life in America, we approached the Metropolis of Hong Kong with tall buildings and bright, colorful lights. I felt like this was a great city to explore.

When we arrived in the city, I thanked him. I found a nice hotel and booked a room. The first thing I did was call my husband.

"Where are you and are you OK?"

We talked for quite a while, and I explained what occurred. He felt relieved.

"Well, you're safe now, so why don't you visit Hong Kong, since you are there?"

I relaxed and slept very well that night.

The next few days after I exchanged my ticket for Seattle, I went on bus trips to Kowloon and back into Mainland China, visiting Macau. In Macau, I visited an old Portuguese church, the ruins of St. Paul, that was being repaired.

On another day, I took a boat ride to visit Victoria Peak, a mountain in the western part of Hong Kong Island. I watched individuals practicing Tai Chi. The topography was lush, and there were clear views of the city skyline. Even the water below was bright blue. The air was crisp on that day.

Even though I only had a few days before I left for Seattle, I experienced quite a bit of exploring the few weeks I was in China. I would return again, I thought, but not solo.

While on the plane to Seattle, I was relieved to be on my way back to the United States, my homeland. I would be in familiar territory with the customs, language, and topography. I felt a bit like Dorothy as she said, "There's no place like home!"

# 14

## UNDER THE DESERT SKY

### SAM NETZBAND

I am sitting in a hot tub listening to the sounds of the creatures of the New Mexican desert. The night sky is full of stars that are amplified by the blackness of the space. Lights are dim or turned off in most homes to preserve the darkness that allows for an illuminated sky.

Allan and I made our way through a weaving grass path to the makeshift spa area. He sprinted ahead of me, more sure of his footing than I. The hot tub was bubbling under the cover. Allan opened the cover, releasing a plume of steam into the relatively chilly air. Even in the desert, nights get cold, especially in October.

Allan found a stool and placed it lightly in front of the hot tub. I kicked off my shoes and threw my towel on a nearby garden bench, folding it as if someone would see the unkemptness. I knew, however, it was just us, the stars, and the creatures of the night. He put out his hand, gesturing for me to hold his as I climbed in. He knows me well, and this small gesture made me smile. I stepped on the stool carefully, praying it wouldn't break, and then, one foot after the other, submerged myself in the blissful warmth of the heated bubbles.

"This is so nice," I whispered, not wanting to wake the hosts of our Airbnb. Allan nodded as he climbed in and sat next to me. We sat in silence, taking in the sky that was open and wide. I saw Orion, a constellation that we'd seen in many of our travels. I couldn't help but wonder if some creature on a star of that constellation ever looked out at Earth and smiled.

The stars shown in the reflection of Allan's glasses. He looked up at the sky in wonder. It amazed me that, after meeting by chance on the internet 5 years ago, we were traveling the world together, continuing to make memories, and that I had now visited all 50 states. Allan must have felt me looking at him. He turned and smiled, and we began our regular banter about pretty much anything under the sun.

# 15

## OUTER SPACED

### MARISSA MONTGOMERY

With a dizzy, awful feeling in my head, I was jolted awake. My inner voice screamed.

"STOP!"

*Night after night, as soon as my head hit the pillow, I could feel my consciousness leave my body. I couldn't stop it. It reminded me of Star Trek—when Captain Kirk would say, "Engage!" The Starship Enterprise would spring forward into warp drive. The stars blurred as ship and crew traveled through the time-space continuum towards their predetermined coordinates. In my case, my mind or spirit—I wasn't sure which part—would slip free of my body, jolt forth at what felt like warp-speed, but without the protective casings of a spaceship or a force-field, without a captain setting a course or destination. Feeling naked and completely vulnerable, I sped through the wall next to my bed, I passed through the exterior of the building out into the night air, and accelerated into the dark sky. The stars blurred as I sped past planets, past the Milky Way and headed to god knows where. Gripped by terror, I wanted it to stop.*

With all my force of will, I tried to pull my consciousness back into my body. Contracting some kind of inner muscle, I jerked up the reigns on the part of me still traveling at warp speed. This inner tug-of-war threatened to tear my mind asunder. Just then, when it became unbearable, the part in outer space retracted like a massive rubber band and snapped back into place, inside my body.

Covered in sweat, I sat up, clutched my head and quietly wept. "No, no, no."

I couldn't lie back down and risk that happening again. Afraid to wake Astrid, my college roommate, I rose from bed, wrapped my comforter around my shoulders and tiptoed out the door and down the hall to the TV lounge, where I curled up on the couch. In the days and weeks following the night Denny assaulted me, the nightmares had become so regular, I gave up on sleep and camped out there. With my stash of Peanut M&Ms, Tab soda, and Marlboro Lights, night after night I held vigil with David Letterman and Agatha Christie.

Eventually, I received a summons from the dean of Student Affairs.

Waking that morning, I wondered, what should I wear? It was unusually warm for the first week of April, so I pulled out the beige linen pants I purchased last summer while cashiering at the candy counter at the department store back home. Carefully ironing a vertical crease down each of the legs, I thought about the mud, the grass stains, the blood I tried to scrub from my sweat pants. Ten minutes later, I donned a light salmon-colored jacket and, alone, set off across campus.

The sky was clear, everything was sprouting, but my spirit had flatlined. Arriving at the campus administrative building, I took the elevator to the third floor where a friendly, middle-aged man waited in the hall to greet me.

"Hi, Marissa, I'm Darren, the dean of Student Affairs." Extending his hand, he directed me toward an office. "Come this way."

Just then, someone I knew slipped past us and onto the elevator without stopping to say hello. It was Jake, the boyfriend of the girl who lived in the room next to mine.

Noticing my confusion, Darren replied. "Here, have a seat. Jake just gave his statement. You may not know this, but he was on his way to visit his girlfriend when he heard your screams. He assumed some drunken students were fooling around, so he didn't intervene. I'm really sorry."

I had nothing to say.

Darren offered me coffee, but I shook my head, knowing I couldn't hold the cup without spilling it.

"We need to wait for the chancellor to call us. As we informed you in the letter, the chancellor called this hearing to determine what happened and whether disciplinary action should be taken. When we go inside, you'll take a seat at the table and I'll sit next you. I'm here to support you. They want to ask you some questions."

Just then, a man opened the door and beckoned us to enter. Awkwardly, I rose to my feet as if some invisible puppeteer lifted my limbs and walked me into the conference room. Denny was seated halfway down a long rectangular conference table. The man who served as our usher took his seat at the end closest to the door. Clearly, he was the note taker. At the head of the table sat an older white-haired man. The scene was strangely familiar. Like my grandfather seated at our family dining table, this man, with his back to us, was looking out the large picture window. He didn't acknowledge my entrance. Finally, turning his chair around, in a cold voice he resumed the hearing.

I was the only woman present. After directing me to a seat positioned directly across the table from Denny, Darren took the seat next to mine. I couldn't look at Denny, so I turned to look out the window at the vast expanse of lawn that stretched from the administration building to the campus's main entrance and fixed my gaze on the deep green shades of spring grass and the neat patterns left by a lawnmower. When someone in the room addressed me, some part of me remained suspended out there in the same flat, emotionless state that had floated me through all the awful episodes of my childhood.

Denny read a written statement he had prepared. My ears started ringing. It was the sound of a siren off in the distance—where was it coming from? Denny was speaking, but I couldn't focus on a word of it.

After he finished, the chancellor asked me to describe what happened that night. With the monotone voice I used to recite the pledge of allegiance, I recounted the sequence of events. "I was about to leave the party, when Denny asked to speak to me..."

When I finished, the white-haired man turned to me with a question. "Marissa, why did you go to the party?"

"I wanted to see my friends."

The chancellor's tone turned critical. "What were you wearing?"

Staring at the lines in the grass, I answered without blinking, without thinking.

"A sweat suit and a jean jacket."

Sitting across from me, I could feel Denny's eyes on me. I still wouldn't look at him, but I sensed his nervous energy.

Denny spoke again, this time with a request. Outside, I could tell the siren was getting close. "Can I ask her some questions?"

Darren turned to me, "Is that alright?"

Without thinking, I said, "Okay." Turning my head, I looked at Denny, I was surprised by his appearance. He was clean shaven, dressed in a wool vest and tweed blazer. For a moment his blue eyes, his blond hair were as striking as ever, but the image was transfigured as soon as his Dennis Quaid smile turned to a grimace.

"Why did you sit in my lap at the party."

"I don't know. I didn't mean to."

At the party, when Denny pulled me onto his lap, I didn't stop him.

He asked me a few more questions, something about flirting and making him jealous. I have no idea how I responded.

When we left the room, Darren apologized. "I didn't know it would go like that."

In a numb voice, I said, "It's okay. I'm okay."

He led me to the elevator. "I'll be in touch as soon as there's a decision."

Walking back to my dorm, I made a detour to the dining hall, where seated alone, I ate a plate of potato chips and chocolate-chip cookies.

Denny was expelled, but no charges were pressed by the school. When Darren called, he said the statements made by the officer and by Mitchell, describing the state they found me in, left the administration no choice.

That was the end of the story.

They didn't contact me again.

I tried to continue my studies, but I quickly spiraled downward until I ended up back in the hospital due to an accidental drug overdose. No one from my family came to see me. At some point my mother found out, because weeks later she complained about the bill. The Sunday after the hearing, when most students on my floor got their weekly calls from their parents, I took the risk of calling home long distance and asked the operator to reverse the charges.

My younger sister, Terrie, answered. "Mommy, it's Marissa, can we accept the charges?"

She paused. "Mommy won't let us talk to you. She's mad. She told me to hang up."

I started crying, "Please don't go."

After that, I stopped going to classes. I stopped taking showers. I didn't care to comb my hair but covered it with a bandana or a baseball hat. In the middle of the week, I walked to the IGA and being 18 years old, the legal age at that time, I purchased a twelve pack of Michelob ponies. Locking myself in my dorm room (a few days earlier, Astrid had moved to another room) I pulled out my poly-sci notebook and sketched pictures of eyeballs, some with tears. I drew storm clouds and lightning bolts, thinking it wasn't that long ago, when I used to draw unicorns in my notebooks. I composed a few lines of melodramatic verse. When I was too inebriated to control the pencil, I sat at my desk and stared out the window at the grassy lawn that stretched all the way to the engineering building. After that, I started partying with a vengeance. Drowning myself in beer, I blacked out a few times. Due to the drug overdose, the administration insisted I see a college drug counselor and put me on probation—any further drug usage would get me expelled.

Meeting in her office on campus, the counselor told me I had to make a choice.

"It's not too late to stop the drinking and the drug use before it gets serious."

She said, "I wasn't an addict yet, but at the rate I was going, I would likely become one."

"The blackouts are a warning."

Given my family history of alcoholism, I wasn't surprised.

She never asked about the incident with Denny and I didn't bring it up. A few months later, I dropped out of school. Denny, despite being expelled, continued his education in Criminal Justice at a more prestigious university.

# 16

## LAS MANOS DE MAMI

### NILSA EVIE MARIANO

*Que linda manita que tiene el bebe*
*Linda Manita-Cancion infantil*

*Translation: What a pretty tiny hand*
*the baby has (Children's folk song)*

It was so obvious how your shoulder dropped, and how you leaned to the side your whole arm under the table. "Mom, are you feeding the dog?" You would straighten up, your hand glistening with the grease of the chicken or pork you had in your hand, licked by the dog. "No, no baby, I no do that." You would smile, your smile beautiful, even with the missing teeth. Our little pug would sit at your feet, waiting for her next bite of food. As soon as I turned my attention away, you were leaning over again.

"Mom, don't feed the dog, please; she should only have her own food." "Yes, honey, ok," and you would continue feeding the dog, convinced that a little meat was good for her.

I remembered the song you used to sing to us when we were little about our baby hands. I asked you to sing it again, so I could review the lyrics. You sang the words. Listening, I tried to hide my tears, because your beautiful soprano voice was hoarse and broken. You waved your hands as traditionally done while singing the tune. These were the same hands you used to feed us, your son and daughter. I gently washed your hands when you were done, in silent thanks.

We were in your home visiting, but you no longer could cook from the wheelchair. Several strokes had left you weak, especially since there was no one there to encourage you to walk. My brother Gil and I lived in New York, opposite ends of the state and you were in San Sebastian, Puerto Rico. Papi was living in Costa Rica. Although you had divorced each other years ago, he continued to urge us to look after you. We failed miserably.

Gilberto had an expensive but small apartment in Brooklyn he had downsized to after his kids moved on. I tried to encourage you to come back with me, that we could get better services and care in the United States. You said no, you wanted to stay there, where they understood you, where you felt safer, where you had your home and one remaining sister.

I tried to make our time together joyful. With my second husband, and your youngest grandchild, we would go to the beach. You loved to watch the water, but more importantly you delighted in watching David, who was 8 years old, play on the beach with the dog or run to you with a seashell he thought you would like. Your aphasia prevented you from speaking long sentences, but you would smile at him so sweetly, that he would run to look for more shells to light up your smile again.

When we returned home, I would go to the kitchen to cook some food. You always expressed your regret that you could not cook for us. I asked if my food was that bad, you would shrug your shoulders and say, "it's okay," as you waved that universal maybe. It was not just due to your legs that you did not cook, but, sometimes you forgot to season or more frightening you often forgot you had something on the stove. This was why you gave up cooking but your hands looked for something to do. We developed a routine, where you set the table, and reminded David to wash his hands, and gave him the dog food to drop into the dog dish. You looked so proud to accomplish these things.

In the morning, or early evening, we sat on the porch, and watched neighbors walk by. You always had a funny comment or just a look, that would set us laughing.

I tried not to think about how you felt when we headed back home. Someone did come in to clean and cook, and sometimes your elderly sister came by, or a neighbor would sit evenings. This is where I failed. I did not insist you come with us, I did not push or fight enough. There were days when it was difficult to care for you. You would get angry at the smallest things, a chair, the plate you were given, the nightgown, the neighbors were loud. You could not help it, but I did not know when or where it would happen. I was a coward. I took over the bill paying, the maintenance of the home. Every summer, we painted the exterior of the house, that showed the effect of daily rains and hot sun. I did this to help you keep the home you loved and that I grew to love as the embodiment of you.

A few years later, I had started a new job, no longer a teaching adjunct, I could not take the whole summer off as I had done several times. We spoke on the phone, meaning, I did most of the talking while you added the few words you could get out. I told you I was coming in 4 days. I had not been to visit you for 4 months. You said okay, and the next day you had another stroke, within 2 days you passed away. I flew out to make the arrangements, full of guilt and shame. I should have been there, I should have taken you back with me, I should have been a better daughter.

Cleaning the house, preparing for the company that would help me pray the novenas in Spanish, I put out the table cloth you loved. You always liked to set a pretty table, and that is a tradition I try to keep. As I smooth out the tablecloth with my hands, I hear your voice telling me to take care of my hands, to not look like a washerwoman. This little tidbit of advice came from your own mother, who, with 13 children, had hired a woman to do laundry. You remembered that this woman's hands were large, wrinkled and chapped. "Don't have those hands, mija," she would say. For that reason, I don't hire myself out for laundry; it's the least I can do for my mom.

The reality is that it is too late to save these hands. They show the years of work that five children, various dogs, and two husbands have leaned into, and my failure to follow Mami's advice. These hands show that what is worth doing, leaves a mark somewhere on our bodies and mind.

Today, setting the table on Thanksgiving Day, I smooth out the tablecloth, arrange the centerpiece and set plates. My hands are chapped, lined, rough, reaching for the lotion I apply it generously over every inch of skin, reconciled that these hands hold memories, both sublime and flawed, that no balm can erase, nor do I wish it, but get the wrinkles please.

# 17

## FAREWELL FAIR FORD

### LINDA LOOMIS

I should not have been surprised when a rusted post-World War II Ford was dragged, screeching and clanking into the garage behind our suburban home one cold autumn Saturday. My son had given me plenty of warning that astonishing events would be part of my life. From the moment he slipped away from me in the delivery room and the doctor announced, "A Boy!" my overwhelming love for him was tempered by a sense of his otherness. I knew he would take me into new territory.

It didn't take long for Jimmy's preference for toy cars and trucks and his love of stories about motorized vehicles to manifest itself. When he was three, he drew a series of large-wheeled cars across my freshly washed and waxed kitchen floor, thinking no doubt that I had moved all the furniture from the room to provide him with an uninterrupted canvas. At five, he heard a radio announcer ask the name of the first car manufactured in Syracuse.

"Tell them it's the Franklin," he said, jumping with excitement.

I sent his answer in on a postcard, and he won two tickets to the auto show for himself and his father. While he was in sixth grade, he built a model Wankel engine and understood how it worked.

By the time he was 14, Jimmy's passion for things mechanical and his reverence for things antique created in him a deep longing for a vintage auto. He sought them out wherever he went. On a drive through the country, he could spot the carcass of a deserted old car enveloped in weeds and well hidden from the rest of us.

"Look!" he'd exclaim, pointing from inside our moving vehicle. "Look over there, past the cornfield. Wow! That's a DeSoto, probably 1935. It could be a beauty with just a little work."

It was with that level of optimism he convinced his father that a 1948 Ford Coupe they'd looked at could take up residence in our garage. Art borrowed a tow truck from the auto dealership where he worked and brought the Ford across town at a cost that depleted our son's entire bank account.

My failure to see the potential splendor that lay beneath dirt, rust, and bird droppings should not be construed as lack of vision. I was only being realistic. Mice nested in the seats; springs poked out through the upholstery; fenders hung askew from their moorings.

"Mom, Mom," Jimmy called as they maneuvered the bulky Ford into the far side of the garage. "Look at this, Mom. She's a beauty."

"What are you ever going to do with it?" I sighed.

"I'm going to fix it up." With that declaration, my son's eyes stared at some distant image that I could not see. Returning to reality, he added, "I'll take you for a drive as soon as I'm 16."

Restoration was on a pay-as-you-go basis. A few weeks of collecting paper route money yielded enough for a trip to the fabric store, where we purchased 15 yards of dove-gray uncut corduroy. Jimmy spent most of that winter tracing patterns from the old upholstery, cutting fabric, and sewing new seat covers on my Singer, which never again could be used for fine stitching. As days lengthened, he rushed to the garage after school to fit, adjust, and secure the new covers.

One spring day, his sisters, father, and I nodded our heads and smiled as we viewed the snug, new seats. We ignored the incongruity of seeing them in what was still a rust heap.

Following his first big accomplishment, Jimmy made steady progress. After offering a few sewing tips, my work was done, but his father provided steady guidance , and even his younger twin sisters were pressed into service. His instructions were clear: "Hold that steady while I drop the solder onto it."... "Pull that bolt out while I've got the jack all the way up."

Step by step, he moved from sanding to filling to buffing to polishing. In addition to learning new skills in auto restorations, he learned to avoid my ire by changing from his work clothes in the basement and washing them separately from the rest of the family clothing. He learned to ventilate the garage before turning on the engine so the fumes didn't drive me out of the kitchen as I prepared dinner.

I learned important lessons, too. I became adept at calculating the volume of snacks I should keep on hand to feed a steady gathering of teenage boys who were drawn to our garage each day to watch the transformation. I learned to appreciate the project for its value in helping them identify problems, find solutions, and conquer challenges. I learned that time is not always linear; in cycles and seasons, those boys grew and changed with astonishing speed.

As he turned 15, then 16, I never wondered where my son was. He was either plodding the streets with his Herald-Journal newspaper bag slung over his shoulder, or he was in the garage spending his paper route money on his car. I watched in wonder, then with pride, as the Ford shaped up.

Jim, as he requested we call him by then, rebuilt the engine, fixed the carburetor, hammered out dents, mounted new brakes, and sanded, undercoated , and painted the body. It passed inspection and was deemed roadworthy, and at last I saw what my son had seen all along. He and his friends drove that Ford all over town. It appeared in the homecoming parade, at the junior prom, and in the driveway of a pretty girl who worked with him at his new after-school job at the library.

We resurrected the old joke about "Ford" being an acronym for "Fix Or Repair Daily" as I was often called upon to provide a gentle push with my Pontiac when the car overheated or stalled. Even though it was restored and running, the amateur mechanics continued to gather for regular repairs, and I stocked ever-growing supplies of cookies and milk. As they grew and changed, so did their conversations—from model rocketry and Boy Scout camp to the price of tickets for the senior ball and the best topics for college application essays.

Eventually, a part-time job at the library and a full-time romance cut into Jim's time with the Ford. Sometimes three or four days passed without his polishing the chrome or checking the oil.

All too soon, he made his college decision, bought a suit for high school graduation, and began the long process of saying the inevitable goodbyes to friends and neighbors. We felt the mixture of excitement and sorrow that comes at such times, times of changing and of casting off in order to move forward.

He told his sister Kate she could have his room when he left, shared his books with his sister Kristin, and gave his boom box to a cousin. He placed a classified ad in that newspaper he had delivered for so many years: For sale, classic car. 1948 Ford coupe restored to near original condition. Runs great.

"That's going to pay for my first year," he said.

People called. One man visited. He said it was his dream to purchase a restored car just like the first one he had driven as a young man. He put money down and set a date for pick up.

On a late summer afternoon, when the slant of sun already promised the coming of autumn, the buyer arrived to pay the balance and take the car. Jim pulled in his jaw and held his lower lip steady as he reached into his pocket for the keys. I saw him caress the roof line as he opened the door for the last time and slid onto the dove-gray corduroy-covered seat. I sensed a slight pause before he engaged the clutch and turned the key. The engine rumbled, and that great midnight blue hulk backed smoothly from the garage down our long driveway.

My son stopped the car. He got out, exchanged a few words and shook hands with the new owner. Then, he reached out and handed over the keys.

"Take good care of her," he said, stepping aside. "She's a beauty."

Jim's father, sisters, and I stood with him and watched as that shiny, smooth-running, 1948 Ford coupe headed down the road, turned the corner, and drove right out of our lives.

# 18

## LOTUS FLOWERS

### KAREN FORESTI HEMPSON

Lotus flowers symbolize our awakening of minds and opening of hearts. Adolescents, like lotus flowers, must navigate through murky waters or turbulent times. If their stems withstand harsh environments and make it to the surface, they blossom with much strength. American youths struggle to figure out who they are. Their continual searches for self-knowledge are interrupted when they encounter hostilities, especially from peers. Self-protection from these hostilities often discourages them from pursuing meaningful relationships. This delays maturity or opening of hearts.

In retrospect, this may explain what happened to me. My adolescent energies were often spent sheltering my sensitivities. Time to blossom and reach out to others came later in life, not during adolescence. Looking back on this painful stage, I recall a mature classmate who willingly risked turbulence to connect with peers.

In a quiet study hall in April of my senior year, I tried to look busy. With college plans in place, we seniors were biding our time and anticipating the end of our 12-year stint.

"What do ya call a mirror that ladies use to put on makeup?"

I glanced up from my notebook. The star quarterback in front of me was turned around, staring at my confused expression with his blue Elvis-Presley eyes. He waited for an answer.

"What? Mirror? What are you talking about?"

*You NEVER speak to me.*

"It's called a vanity," announced his brown-eyed friend from across the aisle.

"Yeah, that's it. Vanity. That's what you have," Blue Eyes said, pointing to me.

I was completely caught off guard. Blind-sided. He rarely spoke to me, so why was he so insulting? I did not understand.

I stammered, "I'm...I'm not VAIN!"

"Yes, you are."

"Why do you say that?"

"Because you never bother to look at anyone."

"That's not true. I look at everyone."

*Besieged.*

Looking away for a moment, I quietly added, "I'm insecure, not vain."

Blue Eyes and Brown Eyes sadly looked at me, "Oh-h."

Why I chose that moment to bare my soul, I will never know. Was it because we were soon parting ways? Maybe Blue Eyes thought that it was his last chance to get to know me, perhaps trying to reach out.

In a pathetic attempt to divert the conversation from my true confession, I blurted, "Are you guys going to the graduation parties? There are about five of them."

"I'm definitely going," said Blue Eyes. "Hey, let's go together."

*Really? I could count on one hand how many times we had spoken in the last 12 years, but okay, going together to parties would be cool. But why now?*

I did not mouth that question. Instead, I agreed to join him, even pick him up in my brother's beat-up 1960 Volkswagen Beetle.

Blue Eyes jumped into the car when I beeped the horn. Zooming to the first party, he slid open the sunroof and let his blond hair blow in the wind. The car's heater was stuck on high, scorching our sandaled feet. Down-shifting, our eyes met when I turned toward him. I smiled, most likely for the first time. The sun reflected his eye color as electric blue.

"Here we are at Mike's graduation party," I announced when I pulled into a driveway, narrowly missing a parked car. Since I parked so close, Blue Eyes struggled to open his door and slip between the two cars. To be polite, I waited for him.

Mike's parents greeted and escorted us to their basement. Red and blue balloons and streamers, our school colors, hung from a low ceiling. It was early. Only a few classmates had arrived. Music by the Doors was blasting from two large speakers.

A boy from my 8th-grade homeroom asked me to dance to "Light My Fire." We started joking like we used to. I forgot how much he made me laugh. Somehow, we lost one another once we entered high school.

Soon the room filled with classmates, and we could hardly move. Conversation and dancing became especially difficult with Jim Morrison thundering like a preacher, "YOU CANNOT PETITION THE LORD WITH PRAYER."

Darkness fell. On to another basement. Leslie Gore's "It's My Party" was booming. Warmed up and feeling good, we seniors embraced on the dance floor, aware that this would be the last time we were together. Unusually tight hugs were exchanged while yelling songs' lyrics. Laughter came easily. We behaved like close cousins.

An hour after the second party, Blue Eyes said, "Let's take a break and visit Jack."

"Uh, sure, why not?"

Jack was another guy with whom I had little association. He was active in the school band and was featured in his band costume in our yearbook. I thought that was a little nerdy.

We headed to a nouveau-riche neighborhood and pulled into a driveway next to Jack's yellow Mercedes. His living room displayed plush wall-to-wall carpeting with a designer sofa and loveseat lying below a contemporary painting. A state-of-the-art color TV and sound system were proudly displayed across the room as its main attractions.

*So, this is how rich kids live.*

Jack no longer seemed dorky in his own surroundings; he was animated and interesting, especially when talking about music. He invited us to sit back and listen to the heavy sound of "In-a-Gadda-Da-Vida," gently dropping the needle onto his pricey turntable. Guitars, drums, and organs merged through large loudspeakers, later breaking into solos. Toward the end of the 17-minute song, we patiently waited for the drummer's solo to end so other instruments could jump back in. The lead singer completed the song with a low, drug-induced, "Yea-ahhh."

We thanked Jack and moved on to another party. Above the VW's engine noise, Blue Eyes asked me where I was accepted to college. Reluctantly, I told him.

"You're going to that college? Why not go to Vassar?"

"Will you fund my tuition?"

"So, what's your major?"

"Math."

I loved my trig teacher. She not only explained hard concepts; she was genuinely cool, yet caring. The morning after Bobby Kennedy was shot in 1968, I showed up in her homeroom searching for answers and some hope that he would survive.

"Gunmen shoot to kill," she said, hardly comforting.

She may not have meant to appear cold. Mathematicians state facts, so she prepared me for the worst. A year later, I learned that she ended her own life with a gun to her head. It took a long time to stop wondering why and accept her irrevocable act.

"Math? What a waste of time," said Blue Eyes, "Why don't you study meaningful stuff like history or literature? I'm gonna write a bestseller."

"Maybe you will someday," I said, rolling my eyes.

"I didn't mean to offend you. Math can't solve problems like the Vietnam War."

"Neither can poems."

Three weeks before we graduated, my best friend's brother was killed in Vietnam. He stepped on a land mine, leaving little of his body for an open casket. I stood before his flag-draped coffin. The dead soldier's mom approached me. We hugged, then stood and stared at what was left of her son.

"I read that the Army makes mistakes when reporting deaths, so I'm waiting for them to inform me that my boy is safe and on his way home."

At 17 years old, I struggled to console this devastated mother.

His death forever changed me. After participating in college war protests, I grew anxious to teach about our nation's past and its disastrous decisions. Blue Eyes was right. I later switched my major to become a history teacher, to embrace the opportunity to teach adolescents the truth. My hope was to help prevent future tragedies like Vietnam. If the next generation grew more civic-minded, they could help our nation progress toward peaceful solutions.

Blue Eyes and I met again at our 20th class reunion. We stood in the middle of the dance floor with former classmates roaming around, searching for familiar faces. He looked professional in his charcoal gray suit, white shirt, and geometric tie. We caught up with one another's lives—we both were married and had daughters.

"I wrote a book, ya know," he stated.

"Really? You said you would."

"Yeah, but it failed." He lowered his eyes and shrugged his shoulders.

"But you still wrote a book. That is a-MAZ-ing."

Would he have admitted failure if we were at our 5-year reunion, a time when we struggled to succeed? Maybe he felt comfortable telling me after I revealed my insecurity two decades ago. I squeezed his hand, smiled, and moved on to greet other classmates whom I hardly recognized.

That was the last time I saw Blue Eyes.

Serving on the 15th class reunion committee, I began tracking down alumni. I learned on Facebook that Blue Eyes had passed away.

*No, that can't be. We're too young.*

At the reunion, I spotted Blue Eyes' senior picture displayed next to photos of deceased classmates. "I read your second book," I whispered to him. It was published while he was on his death bed. I heard that he was able to hold his masterpiece only days before dying.

When I returned home, I longed to remember our youth. In a box filled with old term papers and programs, I located my yearbook. It had not been opened for decades. Braving its old-age odor, I bee-lined to the senior section. Near his picture was Blue Eyes' clever inscription to me, layered in humor:

"May your mathematical endeavors end in brilliant 'failure.' Please go read a book—no—go write one. 'Live, learn, suffer'... no—better yet—do your math homework."

*And yes, Blue Eyes, I did write a book. I wished that I could have shared it with you.*

His obituary stated that he met people with an open heart, like he did when we were young. His successful second book revealed how he stayed true to his willingness to reach out to others, taking a chance even if it meant rejection.

He ended his book by revealing awareness of his imminent death:

"Time was quickly rendering me irrelevant...Writing this book is another way for me to heed Vladimir's warning: Let us do something, while we have the chance! It is my way of remaining involved for another moment or two in this marvelous event called human existence. I do not want to go gentle into that good night. I want to rage against the dying of the light."

Early maturity allowed Blue Eyes to create strong ties in school and throughout life. He became a lotus flower when many adolescents wrestled through murky waters. I wish I could express to him the hard lesson that I learned so many years later.

*Wish I knew how to open my heart then.*

**19**

## PORTRAIT OF A LADY

### FELICIA HAURY

As a child, I had a love-hate relationship with Aunt Louise. I grew up in Los Angeles and loved going to Bakersfield, a rural California enclave, during school breaks. In 1944, the family migrated from Bixby, Oklahoma, to Bakersfield. The family's move to California was a chance for a new beginning with opportunities on a thriving frontier. In her later years, Louise mentioned being sad to have left behind her bicycle, skates, and favorite red peg. I think she brought and carried so much more.

Aunt Louise had eleven children, including a pair of twins who passed away as toddlers. This left six boys and three girls, plenty of kids for me to play with. The two youngest children, Marla and Toby, were my pals. Uncle Tate was Louise's husband and my other pal. He made sure we had fun by taking us on trips to the lake and giving us pocket change for the corner store. When Marla was 13, he allowed her to drive me, Toby, and my sister Sadie around town in the family station wagon. Uncle Tate worked two jobs. He was an orderly during the week at the hospital and, on the weekends, he worked as a gardener. He also kept the yard around their home impeccable.

Meanwhile, Louise kept the inside of the house just as impeccable. It was amazing to me, even as a child, that she was able to keep her home spotless despite having so many children. As the boys got older, Aunt Louise and Uncle Tate converted the garage into a room for them and added a much-needed second bathroom.

Most of what I know about Louise is from stories told to me by my mother. Mama explained that Louise had only one lung due to tuberculosis. In the 1950's, Louise was admitted to a sanitarium for a year, which caused her to be away from her growing young family. When Louise returned home, my mother told me later, children were "all over her." She would have one child in her arms and a couple of them clinging to her legs. What struck me was the one lung. I did not think it was possible to survive with a missing organ. On top of this, I recall Louise smoking and drinking liquor regularly in those days. She had a unique aura that captivated me. Her laugh was a deep-throated cackle, and she had a beautiful smile and mirth-filled eyes. When exercising her raucous laugh, she would throw her head back in glee. Louise was tall, thin, and sturdy with golden tan skin. Her hair was soft and curly, and she usually wore it in a small afro framing her oval face. Her most endearing feature was her southern drawl, which was incongruous to a California inhabitant.

I admired Louise but also feared her. Part of the secret to keeping her house clean was that she made all the children stay outside during the day under threat of punishment if we came inside. I was usually there in the summer, so it meant enduring scorching heat. We learned quickly where to find shade outside, usually under the two backyard apple trees where we amused ourselves playing cards and eating the apples as snacks.

The death of my great-aunt Louise marked the end of an era. She was the last surviving member of her immediate family, which included my great-grandparents, called Mama Tig and Daddy Roe, their two sons Roy and Mike, and two daughters, my grandmother Fay and Louise. Louise passed away in July 2022.

Aunt Louise loved horses. She befriended a local rancher in Bakersfield who owned a corral. After observing her interaction with the horses, the farmer allowed her to ride them whenever she wished. At her funeral service it was mentioned that she had a gentle way with these majestic animals and would talk to them as if they were human.

Another story a family friend told during the service was Aunt Louise and her siblings' love of riding motorcycles. It was said one of them always had a broken limb at any given time. My grandmother, Fay, was among these riders. This set of siblings grew up in Oklahoma's Indian Territory. I would love to know what they were like before migrating. Louise's obituary has multiple photographs of her with horses and on motorcycles. At the mausoleum a horse stood sentry as a symbol of respect while she was interred.

## Louise's Final Journey

"Grandma wasn't mean, she was crazy," stated her great-granddaughter at Aunt Louise's funeral service. The teen told a story about when she was a little girl and scraped up some money to buy herself some Hot Cheetos. She offered some to her Grandma Louise, warning her that they were hot. Louise tried one with no expression. The great-granddaughter left the room and when she returned, the bag of chips was empty.

Aunt Louise also suffered from dementia. One friend recalled Louise driving too far from home once and not remembering how to return. She sought help from an officer who had her follow his cruiser back home. Louise is said to have found this incident funny. Not because she got lost but because there was an angry line of drivers honking as they tried to get around her. They were compelled to follow behind her when they saw the police car ahead of her.

A photograph flashed on repeat on the video projector at Aunt Louise's funeral. It showed her standing deep in thought standing at her kitchen window. She had a faraway look in her eyes. She was thin and frail with thinning gray hair pulled into a ponytail. I wonder if she was thinking of her three sons who predeceased her or childhood in Oklahoma. Aunt Louise had stopped drinking and smoking and was active in her church during her later years. Perhaps she was communicating with God. The kitchen I always remember as being spotless is in the background. After meals there was no evidence that food had been recently prepared as the stove was always clean and the counters were clear of dishes and clutter. I envisioned the converted garage one room over and the line of beds for her boys covered in plain dark blankets like military barracks. The kitchen window is where Aunt Louise kept watch over Mayfair Street. A place where she yelled at the neighborhood kids to stay off her lawn. A neighbor shared at the funeral how Aunt Louise loved her blue truck, and everyone knew when she backed out of her driveway to get out of her way. She would drive slowly, oblivious to the kids playing in the street, anxious to return to their games.

After Aunt Louise's funeral service, interment and repast, family and friends slowly gathered in her backyard on Mayfair Street. She had lived a month shy of her 88th birthday. Adults sat at card tables and benches smoking, drinking, and playing cards or dominoes. Her great-great grandchildren ran in circles around the house. A huge shade tree sat in the middle of the yard, a tree that did not exist when I was growing up. The apple trees were gone. Louise's daughter, Laila, emerged from the back door eerily mirroring her mother's gait and temperament. She sat at a bench with me as we dodged bees buzzing around our heads attracted to the sweet, canned soda. After a while she got up and started yelling to her young nieces, "Y'all better watch your children. If I punish 'em, you gon' be mad at me. You're lucky I'm not drinking any Jack Daniels!" I don't think she realized at that moment how much she sounded like her mother. My cousin Marla invited me to a game of dominoes. I had to decline because I didn't know how to play. I was so inspired by this scene that when I returned home, I bought myself a set of dominoes to learn how. Ultimately, I saw Louise as a multifaceted person leaving an indelible mark on our family. The little girl who had to leave her favorite red peg, skates, and bicycle in Bixby, Oklahoma.

# 20

## "I Am Too Damn Old"

### Indu Gupta

She was a frail, tall and slender woman in her late 70s. She always walked in with a big smile on her face and straight back without any imbalance every 3 to 4 months for routine check ups in my medical office. Her blood pressure, heart rate, and the rest of the physical exam were normal for her age. She was a retired accountant as I recall. I learned she had not found a right person to marry and did not desire a companion. She was content with her life. Initially, she came by herself. I don't remember if she drove or someone accompanied her. Her brain was sharp, and she complied with all my recommendations. We enjoyed each other's company during her 20- to 30-minute check-ups.

"Margaret, you are doing great. I will see you in three months. Make sure to call me if you have any problem," I would remind her at the end of the visit.

But she always got the last word.

"Doc, you know what my problem is? I am too damn old!"

She would open the exam room door with big ear-to- ear smile showing her teeth and with bright eyes peeking through big glasses, She always left me speechless. I would smile back and try to rebut.

"You are great, keep up the good work!

After a year or so, she was using a cane when she came to my office. Nothing else changed. Same spunky, larger-than-life personality, which put me in awe of her. She did not make fuss about needing a cane, but I started to get concerned because with time we all can get frail. She lived alone and had no other activities. To my surprise, I learned she was not a social person. I encouraged her to walk and keep her muscles moving and have nutritious, plentiful food. We discussed if she felt she is doing okay at home or if she needed any help. She was quick to respond.

"I am good, no worries. My nephew John takes care of my needs for groceries and appointments. He is like my son."

I suggested she consider physical therapy, but she was not interested. Since she had no falls, aches, or significant arthritis pain in any knee or hip point, I did not push it further. During her follow-up visits that year, she seemed to be losing some weight and looked more frail. Her exam and lab tests again were all fine. She had had no falls and did not have symptoms of depression. She did not have any financial constraints, she had assured me.

But I started to see that she was getting lonely, and was mostly limited to her house with no friends or family other than her nephew, John, who was now a consistent and reliable presence in her life. I met him during a visit a year later. He wheeled her in a wheelchair from the parking lot to the waiting area. I was worried and showered her with many questions. She replied with the same wittiness.

"Doc, nothing is wrong with me. John wants to meet you so here he is. You know I am too damn old!"

I asked her questions, and examined her. She looked frail, had lost a few pounds, and her skin had lost elasticity indicating she was not drinking enough water. Her muscle strength was lower than I would expect. I did not detect any obvious abnormality during the thorough examination. She had no neurological abnormalities. She was able to stand by herself from the wheelchair, and taking a few steps was possible, though wobbly. She declared she was still making her meals and did not use the wheelchair at home. John mentioned she needed the wheelchair because the distance from the parking lot to the elevator and then the long hallway would be too far for her to walk. That made sense so I did not argue or protest. Once more, I recommended lab tests and she agreed. I asked if she would consider an aide at home. I encouraged her to consider having an evaluation of her home for safety and get physical therapy at home, since John was not available to transport her to biweekly or weekly therapy sessions, and other transportation would be costly. John encouraged her to accept my recommendations and, to my surprise, she said okay. I realized she knew her limitations.

Before the conclusion of the visit, she declared, "Doc, I will never go to any assisted living or nursing home. I want to stay in my own home and will die where I have lived for almost 80 years!"

John agreed with her and said he will help her as much as she needs because he loves his favorite aunt. I smiled and promised her that I would do everything I could to help her age graciously with dignity at home. But, I told her, she will need to eat better, not skip meals, and follow all my and John's recommendations.

She winked and said with the familiar smile, "Yes Doc! I know my problem is...? We both said it together in a chorus. " I am too damn old!"

John pushed her wheelchair out to the reception area, made a follow-up appointment, and coordinated a home evaluation by a nurse to assess home safety and need for physical therapy.

The home-care nurse went to her house and met Margaret and John. She created a thoughtful home-care plan that was acceptable to everyone, especially Margaret. The assigned visiting nurse was thorough during her follow-up home visit with Margaret as well and made sure that the physical therapy evaluation was done on time. She would always call my office with any concerns. We worked together to resolve issues by coordinating proposed solutions. We became a strong support system for Margaret and she continued to stay at her home as she had wished. She enjoyed her freedom in her home, which she called her heaven.

A year passed. One Monday morning around 7 AM, I was getting ready to go the hospital to make hospital rounds before starting my office to see scheduled patients, my pager went off. In those days, we had pagers tucked in our belts or the pockets of our white coats to receive messages from the answering service. We would call the person back who requested the return call. That morning it had come from the hospital's emergency department. I was annoyed because I would be late for the office. Most likely, I thought, someone had come in a few hours earlier and needed to be hospitalized. I called the ED, and the charge nurse picked up the phone.

"Hi, this is Dr. Gupta. How can I help you?"

The nurse replied, "Oh, Dr. Gupta, your patient Margaret is here. You know, your 80-year-old, very frail looking lady. You need to see her before she can be transferred to the nursing home."

My heart sank, my hand stopped as I was putting my eyeliner.

"What happened? No one called me overnight. I was on call. Who decided that she should go to the nursing home?"

With every question, I became more agitated, but bit my tongue.

The nurse on the other end of the phone understood. We had known each other for years through regular interactions in the ED.

There was silence, then she quietly said sympathetically, "Dr. Gupta, I don't know the details. I just started the shift at 7 AM and was given this hand off from the overnight shift with the message that a visiting nurse had gone to her home and saw how frail she was."

The charge nurse continued, "Margaret had no complaints, but the new visiting nurse insisted that she was not safe to stay at home and called 911. The ambulance brought her to the ED. In fact, Margaret told the nurse that she is fine but needs assistance with everyday chores.

She is neither confused nor did she have any falls. The night ED doc saw her and made a referral to a social worker for home safety. That social worker assessed her and concluded that Margaret was not safe for discharge to live by herself at home and recommended a nursing home placement for her day-to-day needs."

I was stunned! I said thank you and hung up. I had a lump in my throat and a feeling of impending doom mixed with disappointment and sense of defeat. I rushed to the ED. The charge nurse pointed me to the large boarding area where multiple patients were parked from overnight shift. Many of them were waiting for their next destination, mostly not of their liking. I slowly walked toward Margaret's bed, which was at the end of that holding area. I pulled the curtain to get some privacy. She was sitting upright with the support of a pillow. Her face looked pale and neck was slightly slumped forward as if it did not want to hold her head. Her lips were tightly closed and eyes had no twinkle. She did not say a word but her eyes did. I felt like a little girl who had disappointed a beloved aunt. I was sad, disappointed, and angry. After a few minutes, I thought, "I am her doctor and she is looking at me and probably thinking... could you do something to stop this!"

I pulled myself together and softly asked, "Margaret, how are you ? What happened?"

Her long, thin face looked even longer, her lips quivered, and her eyes were watery.

"Doc, what happened? Age happened, you know what my problem is. I am too damn old!"

Tears started to flow down her cheeks. I started crying and embraced her tightly. We both wept.

I evaluated her; as always, she was sharp with all her mental faculties. Her exam was normal except she was frail. She knew it well but she could not do anything to stop it. Neither could anyone.

"Let me find out more," I said.

Margaret nodded as if she knew nothing could happen now. I went back to the nurses' station and asked to speak to the social worker who made this cold life-changing decision for Margaret, giving her a life sentence of imprisonment against her will. I was told that it was the night social worker and her shift was over. In addition, adult protective services had gotten involved.

"She is not safe at home," concluded the protective services who had spoken with Margaret's nephew, who did not object, I was told by the day shift's case manager, who was coordinating a nursing home transfer. I thought her nephew John did not or could not dare to object. I contemplated.

"Dr. Gupta, she is accepted in a nursing home so she can leave soon once you okay it."

"Did you ask Margaret?" I questioned.

"The patient was told she was being moved to a nursing home and did not have any questions," the case manager replied politely, seeing the frustration, sadness, and anger evident on my face.

"She does not want to go to a nursing home. What can I do to stop it?" I asked, almost pleading with her.

"Sorry, Dr. Gupta, nothing you can do now will stop this. Adult protective services and a social worker deemed her unsafe to stay alone. Since she is in the hospital, the hospital will not discharge her to home. Her nephew does not live closer to her. It is all too risky. The nephew did not want to take on a big responsibility like this and he agreed that she should receive 24/7 care," the case manager continued. "Unless she wants to sign out against medical advice, which she does not want to do," she added.

I knew Margaret did not have any strength or will left to fight a powerful system. It was like David and Goliath, I thought. No one including John will ask her to sign out against medical advice.

"You should ask the ED doctor who evaluated her and ask him to make the decisions for discharge to the nursing home."

I was visibly upset and was trying to control my tears. "It is not my place to stop or discharge her. I do not agree with this assessment and decision whoever made it, but unfortunately, I am helpless and as powerless as Margaret," I replied.

I walked toward her room. She was sitting in the same position as I had left her. She had not touched her breakfast tray. She looked at me.

"I am so sorry, Margaret." I started to cry. "I understand that John spoke with the social worker and everyone else and they think you will not be safe at home." I continued with a hopeful message, "Let's have a plan. You take this opportunity to get stronger, eat and drink well, exercise every day and you can go back to your home sweet home. One of my patients of your age just did that. It was great. Can you promise me not to give up? You can call me, too, even though I do not work at the nursing home, I can always talk to you on the phone."

I was trying my best to give her hope, but I could see that it was not working. She was quietly listening to me. I held her hand and embraced her one last time. We both were weeping.

I quietly left her room and the emergency department and walked to my office. Margaret was a casualty of a well-intended system that forced its will on her with the intent to protect her well being, but in reality it caused immense harm.

I was already late for my first office appointment, which is un-like me, who always took pride in honoring timeliness in keeping appointment times for every patient the majority of time, except during unexpected situations like today or if a patient presents with illness during a routine office visit. I rushed through the door.

"How are you?" my longtime secretary, Lydia, asked. She had become like family; we worked extremely well together.

"Not well," I replied in a shaky voice.

"What happened?"

She got worried. I explained Margaret's situation quickly and got teary.

"You know, Lydia, this is very unfair. How dare strangers make such a drastic decision for her life? I don't think Margaret can survive there. I am so worried, but I feel so helpless."

Lydia agreed and tried to comfort me.

My first patient was in the exam room and I slowly started my day. I thought about Margaret at times, and hoped that she might accept her new home and one day call to let me know how she was doing.

A month has passed. One afternoon, I was sitting in my office, catching up on paperwork. Lydia entered my office and stood silently. I looked up and took a break from a pile of overdue paperwork she had given me for signatures.

"Give me a few more minutes, and you will have it soon," I told her with a grin. Lydia did not say a word and stood quietly.

"What, did something bad happen?" I asked with concern.

"Yes," she replied in a soft voice. "Margaret passed away. I read her obituary last night. I am so sorry," Lydia looked at me as if she was trying to comfort me.

"Oh."

I lost my words. After a few minutes of silence, I replied as if I was trying to comfort myself.

"She is finally at peace now."

Tears flowed down my cheeks and started to wet the insurance forms on the table waiting for my signature. I felt deep sadness and relief at the same time. Margaret cannot suffer any more! I closed my eyes to pray and also to control my tears. Few minutes later, I wiped my eyes with facial tissue and started to complete those forms that Lydia had asked me to complete.

Margaret could not help herself but prepared me to fight against this unjust forced decision by a health system for anyone else. After Margaret's passing, I learned vigorously about patients rights, discussed different situations with social workers, case managers, and advocated successfully for other patients during their most vulnerable times alongside their families, so no one can ever displace any Margaret from her beloved home against her wishes.

I still miss Margaret.

# 21

# WESTCOTT WINTER

SAMUEL D. GRUBER

Winter is here. The neighborhood has shut down. Trees are bare, exposing the houses, but there are few people on the street to see them. Winter is welcome when it comes, opening the door to the holiday season, but here in Syracuse, the cold and dark linger overlong.

December is still festive, with lights and decorations on houses, and people moving to holiday parties. When doors open, the sounds of talk, laughter and music filter out. For the past 25 years until the pandemic, I've hosted a Chanukah party every December. The party kept growing, along with the children for whom it was originally intended. Soon, in the way of many holiday parties, it became impossible not to have it. Depending on the severity of the weather, the mountain of boots in the entryway can be almost as high as our spirits. People are not just happy to eat and drink; they are relieved. Westcott, where I live, has evolved into a university district, so for a good many residents there is a combined sigh and groan that marks the semester close. Classes end, let the parties begin.

Mine has always been a local party, but I tweak the Chanukah story depending on my mood and the world political situation. It started so my Jewish children could entertain their mostly not-Jewish friends, and for me to educate my neighbors about the value of potato latkes, applesauce, corned beef, and brisket. Fifty years ago, this would not have been necessary. This area was a center place for Syracuse's Jewish population, a waystation on the Exodus from Downtown to the nearby suburbs just over the city line.

The crop of children who sit cross-legged on the living room floor to hear my story of Chanukah changes every few years. As I talk on, they impatiently wait to light one of the many menorahs, their chance to play with fire. Academics are a transient species, so many adults, too, come for a few years, and then they also disappear. My children are now adults, and they've gone too.

One year, when the party made the front page of the Syracuse paper, a friend from Spain was pictured filling her plate from a laden table. She was thrilled, but her strict Catholic mother back in Spanish Galicia was highly displeased. Matilda's hometown had not achieved Westcott's level of ethnic diversity and ecumenicalism. Since Chanukah usually comes earlier than Christmas, another family always arranged to have their family photo for their holiday card taken at the party. Since Annetta is Polish, she knows all about potato pancakes.

Mine is just one of many holiday parties. For about 2 or 3 weeks, the street is filled with parked cars near houses shining with light. People walk gingerly clutching casseroles, wine bottles, and bags filled with beer. One friend had a Christmas cookie decorating party for many years. Another, a party to make tree ornaments. Still another has a big potluck, which is preliminary for all the diners to head out—a music booklet in hand—to sing carols. If it all seems idyllic, it really is. It all lasts until just after New Year's, and then there is silence.

Trees go up early here. Through December, they are lit up in downstairs windows visible at twilight. My wife had no religion, but was patiently tolerant of most others, and she loved all holidays of light. One of our last happy pictures together was when we posed, draped with strings of lights at a local Diwali celebration. In her Italian American family, the tradition was to get the tree just before Christmas, decorate it on Christmas eve, and then keep it up into January. We tried that the first year we moved to Syracuse and could hardly find a tree. But unlike in New York City, where we bought our tree on the street corner, here we could go to a tree farm and cut one down.

I easily accepted the tree since there was no theology with it, but it took me some time to appreciate Christmas lights, or holiday lights as they increasingly are known. But why not? Every culture has its holiday of light: Christmas, Chanukah, Solstice, Diwali. In deep December we all crave more light. Electric Christmas lights developed on the same timeline as this "streetcar suburb." Thomas Edison and Edward H. Johnson were the first to show off a string of electric lights in 1880 in Menlo Park, just about the time the Hillsdale Housing Tract—where I live—was imagined. In 1903, at about the same time the first houses on nearby Allen Street were going up, Edison's General Electric Company began to offer pre-assembled kits of Christmas lights. Like the automobiles at the time, however, stringed lights were for the well-to-do or the home engineer. Wiring lights was expensive and required a "wireman," what we call an electrician today. Possibly, some Allen Street houses put up lights in the early years of the century. Both electricity and gas were included when they were built.

In 1923, 3 years after my house was built, President Calvin Coolidge flicked a switch and lit up the National Christmas Tree near the White House, and then the nation took notice. The tree had 3,000 electric lights , and it didn't burn down. Coolidge, who didn't do much else in his presidency, showed the country the potential of electric decoration.

In the 1920s, American cities and especially suburbs did not suffer much from light pollution. Except maybe in a theater district, you could step outside and see the stars. In a residential area like mine, there were few streetlights or car headlights to illuminate the scenes. Nights could be very dark, and starry skies very clear.

The introduction of colored Christmas lights must have drastically changed the outdoor experience, at least for a few weeks of the year. Now I wish that people would leave their lights up much longer to get us through the dark days. A few people do. With the introduction of new white lights, icicle lights, and inexpensive LED lights, we string electric lights ever deeper into January and February, and even year-round. There are strings of lights and lit wreaths over doorways, on porches, and around bushes and tree trunks, too. I use them as guideposts on dark nights to find my way home. They are part of a millennia-old movement to chase away the long dark nights.

My bedroom faces the street. There is a polygonal bay window that pushes out, with its angled sides designed to catch the maximum daylight from different directions. That works fine when the sun is up, but at nighttime it wants to keep working, funneling light it collects from streetlights, a half-moon, or car headlights onto my bed, into all hours. The big window collects sound, too. Clarke Street is relatively quiet , but car sounds, pedestrians returning from late-night revels, the occasional dog bark, and other sounds shoot through the thin cold night air into my bedroom. Over time, however, rhythms of light and sound join the rhythms of body and mind. I can ignore most of the disturbances. I expect others do the same.

It gets dark early in winter and stays dark late. It's hard to tell time just by the light. This morning, I open my eyes fully awake, but my body knows it is still too early. My phone says 4:00 AM, but outside it is bright as day. It's been snowing, and there is a bright night glow under the streetlights. Outside , snow wraps everything, erasing the lines between houses, driveways, lawns, sidewalks, berms, and streets. Trees and cars are covered under a great white mass, emanating a gentle glow like a lantern. Around the houses the light is murky and a little gray, but across the lawns and streets there is a whiteness as sharp and loud as a xenon arc-lamp.

I take in the silent scene and go back to sleep. By six, however, out of silence begins the chirping of the sparrows huddling in the hedges even though all the leaves are gone. Their chatter gets louder and louder as my ears adjust. Then I hear the first scrapes of shovels on the concrete sidewalk. Someone on Clarke Street is out. The shovel sounds a clarion call, loud and raucous, but more rhythmic and sustained than the cawing of the crows , which sometimes mark the winter pre-dawn.

Just a few years ago, the first shovel scrapes would be joined by others as more neighbors were roused. By the time I'd have my coffee and don my boots, we might have been half a dozen, clearing walks and driveways, getting the car out for work and the kids to school. There was camaraderie in all this. We would salute each other; a moment of warmth that made me perversely welcome the snow. It still happens, but less often.

Now, there is also the whir of blowers that rises in pitch as they throw snow ever higher onto embankments, but when the spray falls, it makes no sound. Do-gooders use their blowers to clear the sidewalks of the entire block. They make fast work of our 40-foot lengths of sidewalks. This is a great for me, and other aging neighbors, but the itinerant shovelers, who really need the money, now must hustle to get there first. Blowers leave an inch of snow on the pavements. When that melts and freezes again, every surface is slicked with treacherous ice. My step on ice is a little less certain as I grow older. Only a good shovel scrapes the concrete.

Soon comes the crash of the plows; high and precise for pick-up truck plows just clearing a driveway, or raucous, clanging, and booming if a big city-operated plow. These charge down the street like marauding mechanical mastodons. Their broad, curved plows hang low, raised just slightly above the surface as they race from place to place, or let down close, to scrape the snow and ice of the road with a screeching fury as they careen through. The trucks must drive fast for the most powerful scrape and push. The drivers mostly seem to know what they are doing; they can maneuver with balletic delicacy, though I have seen this dance shift quickly into a demolition derby. Woe to the car parked in the wrong place, or to the just-cleared driveway apron, now filled with heavy snow pushed from the road. This plowed snow is the breaker of backs. If left for just a little while, it freezes as hard as the Wall of Ice that protects the Seven Kingdoms in the *Games of Thrones*.


The parties are over, and the dark and cold have settled in for a Syracuse winter. All movements are bundled, the streets are hushed, and January moves in slow motion. In the long, cold months, it is sometimes hard to believe people live here at all. The houses and streets go into half-hibernation.

The quiet can be a blessing. When January and February are very cold, the sun shines for much of the day, and with proper cold weather gear, it is bracing to walk. Snow squeaks when it is dry and it blows away when it is "Lake Effect." I push forward in the deep wet accumulation after a real blizzard and light-headed from sucking in the cold air that stabs deep into my sinuses, clearing a passage as effectively as hit of wasabi. For some, the dark and cold are a depressant, and they flee to warmer climes. For me, at least for now, winter is a testing tonic (I just hope it ends before April).

# 22

## THE WRITERS

### MARY C. GILLEN

I f we're lucky, as writers, we'll have a day when we are gifted with a blessing and another time when we're regifted with the same blessing. For me, that gift and its second giving went unrecognized and unappreciated for decades. It was easier to see the barricades.

In 2023, at the age of 83, I enrolled in a memoir class through the Downtown Writers Center at the YMCA of Central New York. I was scrambling to come up with some material for a class assignment. Due, of course, that evening. I dug through boxes packed from several previous moves. In one of them, lying on top of heaps of outdated papers, was a flat, straw-like hanging mat with the word LETTERS printed in red on an attached pocket, along with a Snoopy cartoon. The letter holder and the cartoon were gifts my mother gave me over 35 years ago. Tucked inside the pouch were two of my published articles from the 1990s. And my haiku poem from the Haiku Society of America edition, fish in love.

I also found a spiral notebook titled THE HORTENSE BOOK, in my mother's handwriting. Inside the back cover were my 25 word-for-word typed pages of its transcription.

Recovering these treasures was a gift. Rereading my mother's stories stirred up many memories for future classes. They also gave me a lot more.

One morning in 1988, while living in Pennsylvania, I sat at my desk after sending my two middle schoolers off for the day. My mother, Hortense Miriam Shea Gillen, placed a brown paper bag next to my green electric typewriter. I was 48, and Mom was 88.

I looked up from the story I was working on, aware that she was standing beside me. I was positive she gave me something to "help improve my housekeeping skills," a topic that arose whenever she visited for a week or two.

"You always have a book in your hand. How do you expect to get anything done?" was this week's mantra.

Opening the bag, I took out the straw mat, its red letters a bit faded.

"Letters? Mom, is this to hold my outgoing mail?"

"No, you told me you submitted poems and articles to magazines." She rubbed her fingers over the empty bag. "I got this for your acceptance letters."

She remembered? I was flabbergasted to use one of her favorite words. My mother and I had a competitive, uneasy relationship, filled with what I felt was her belief of how I should do things. I was often bewildered by how she set the tone, and how we worked against each other.

I have to admit that I contributed to this tension. I lived inside an iron container filled with fear and guilt, trying to convince myself that I was bisexual, that I could overcome my desire to return to the gay community. And dreading that someone would "out me." I stared at Mom, leaned back in my chair, then looked at her gift.

"I couldn't find a holder labeled WRITER," she said. "So, I got this one. I put a Snoopy cartoon in the pocket."

It was a panel she had clipped from her local newspaper weeks before. I read it silently, anticipating a sharp message indicating that I needed to work harder, faster, neater, or...?

But there was Snoopy. The World's Most Famous Writer, reading a harsh rejection notice from editors who threatened to throw rocks at his mailbox because of his writing.

"Another form rejection slip," Snoopy says, tossing the letter over his shoulder with a dismissive flourish.

It took me several seconds to realize the cartoon was not a jab at me. Paired with the straw holder for my acceptance letters, it was a show of my mom's support. It took another moment to absorb this gesture before I could thank and hug her. Mom's shoulders relaxed. Then I allowed mine to ease. We met one another's eyes with tentative, then amused smiles that said "Truce."

"What do you think, Mare?" She moved a bit closer to my desk.

"I love them, Mom," I said, holding the gifts up for a closer look. My heart squeezed with a deep, deep desire to stuff that pouch with acceptance letters until it burst. At the same instant, a bee-buzz in my head reminded me that I was incapable of quality writing. That I could never compare to my two older male cousins. In our family, they were considered "The Writers," "The Untouchable Geniuses."

Mom and I read the cartoon out loud, laughed over Snoopy's cavalier approach to rejection. We admired his determination to keep on writing what he liked, his beloved novel, It Was a Dark and Stormy Night.

After a brief pause, she mentioned the short story correspondence course I was taking with the Writer's Digest University.

"I read the two stories you sent me," she said. I held my breath. "They're really good."

I exhaled. Oh my God! She complimented me, not her "If only you would have..." speech.

I held that compliment as if it were a living thing. I hugged her again. Tighter this time.

This started me thinking that maybe my mother did believe that I could be a writer.

I began to recognize Mom had language skills beyond reading noir and hard-boiled stories by the Golden Age of Detective Stories authors. Raymond Chandler's protagonist, Philip Marlowe, was one of her favorites. The Four Queens of Mysteries, Agatha Christie, Dorothy Sayers, Ngaio Marsh, and Margery Allingham, were at the top of Mom's list. Then there were 60 years of continuous letter correspondence to friends. Maybe this was why my cousins valued her input.

To the best of my recollection, years ago, my cousin Robert would have her read and comment on drafts of his published novels. My cousin Marguerite, a prolific writer and reporter for a newspaper, would run ideas by her for articles. Then there was my cousin George, "the playwright," who spent hours on the phone with Mom. Since they were always honor-roll students compared to my barely passing grades, I believed they never doubted their talents nor did they struggle.

What an eye-opener and brain-shaker that three professional, college-educated writers sought my mother's input, despite her having left high school at 16 to attend secretarial school. At that time, I didn't grasp her capabilities.

For years, our family prodded and urged Mom to write her life story. Mom's response was a faraway look and a quick shake of her head. For her 82nd birthday in 1982, she accepted a bright red 70-page notebook with a label titled "THE HORTENSE BOOK."

"There's not a lot I can write. A postcard will do," she said.

In early 1987, Mom returned her memoir to us, which was 3-quarters filled with her handwriting and signature, dated from 1982 to 1985.

"You changed your mind. How come?" We all wondered.

"I realized that I'm the only one left. I was the eighth of eleven children," she said. "At one time, there were us kids, my parents, and four tenants living in that Greenwich Village brownstone."

I slid a cup of tea to her.

"If I don't record things, there's no one else left to do so," she said. "Not even cousins." She stirred the tea with her spoon, looking sad.

I wanted to know: "Did you include that you were an assistant deputy sheriff? You know, when you did administrative work for that big shot congressman?" This was my favorite story.

"Oh yeah, I still have the badge," she said with a sly smile. "I enjoyed reminiscing. So many beautiful memories. I've really lived a lot, haven't I?"

Let's go back to 1988. Mom and I sat at my kitchen table and read some of her eight thousand-plus words, which she had handwritten despite her arthritis.

"I gave my typewriter away years ago," she said, holding up her misshapen fingers. "It was slow going, Mare, slow going."

Side by side, with cups of tea, The Hortense Book, Agatha Christie novels, and with the Snoopy cartoon, we were two companionable writers and avid mystery story fans.

Before I drove her home from Pennsburg, PA, to Lynbrook, NY, we hammered a nail into the wall above my desk and hung the "Acceptance Only" mat. We attached the Snoopy cartoon to the front of the pouch. Snoopy was not only the World's Most Famous Writer but also had the moniker of The World's Most Famous Detective and Most Famous Spy. He was the perfect choice.

"There!" Mom said, stepping back and folding her arms.

During our 4-hour ride, true to our pattern, the atmosphere shifted from friendly to prickly—like a cactus—with underlying frustrations resurfacing. To use another of Mom's favorite words—"It was exasperating!"

Despite that disappointment, I drove home thinking about opportunities for women authors from the 1920s through the 1990s. I wondered if my mother could write a police procedural or detective story. I could picture her as the protagonist.

Eight years later, at the age of 96, Hortense Miriam Shea Gillen suffered a massive stroke while living at the Regency Apartments in Syracuse, NY. She was confined to a nursing home until she passed away in July of 2001 at the age of 100 years, 7 months.

I had lost my partner in pursuing new mystery and crime stories and rehashing the plots of the Four Queens of Crime. Sometimes recoiling from the dark stories of the noir and hard-boiled series.

By 2001, two of my older cousins had passed away, and the third no longer wrote. The essence of their art continues in their written words. It is a family legacy I strive to continue.

My mother encouraged me to write when I was 8 years old. It was April 1948 when the first crime drama show made its debut on TV. The show was titled "The Police Reporter," and featured Barney Blake as the lead newspaper reporter. I was enthralled by Barney's expertise and had dedicated myself to becoming a greater reporter than Barney.

One rainy summer afternoon, Mom set up a TV table to hold her 1930s black portable typewriter and a Webster's Dictionary. She showed me how to roll a sheet of paper into the carriage. Then she spent the entire afternoon helping me spell words and calling encouragement from the kitchen. "You're doing a good job, Mare, keep going."

Mom became my sweetest, funniest, and most compassionate friend ever. Then again, she couldn't remember much of the past. Each visit after her stroke became a renewed beginning, a new friendship.

On the days when I find it daunting to write two words, I remember three things:

1. What my mother wrote in her HORTENSE BOOK, "I think this really does it. I am getting writer's cramp. I have already worn out one pen." Then she found a new pen and wrote an additional 278 words.

2. Snoopy tossing off rejection slips with confidence. There's a 2004 WRITER'S DIGEST book titled Snoopy's Guide to the Writing Life. It is a compilation of responses from 30 world-famous writers and entertainers to Snoopy's "at the typewriter" strip. This is one of my favorite books.

3. Most often, I remember my mom rolling the sheet of paper into her typewriter. And hearing her repeat, "Write, Mare! Just write!"

# 23

## School Lunches

### Vincenza Freeborn

When I think about my school cafeteria, it's not the food, or the old lunch lady monitoring the room, or the clicks of students claiming their reserved tables that I recall. I remember the dread that consumed me all morning, worrying that I didn't have enough money for lunch. I counted the change in my pocket so no one would see me counting. I knew the shape and thickness of quarters, dimes and nickels. I counted repeatedly, over and over, all morning, even though I knew my mother had given me enough money for lunch.

At school, with my friends and mostly, non-friends, I could not bear to have that feeling of shame that I had in the grocery store when judging smirky eyes glared at my mother when she used food stamps. I could hear pity when they sucked their teeth and feel hate when they'd breathe their sighs. I know my mother worried, even though she used a clicker to add up the cost of the groceries as she put them in the cart. At school, I had no clicker to assure me that I had enough money. I could feel the line of kids behind me, waiting for one sign or mistake that would expose my poverty and ignite their cruelty.

# 24

## REGRETS

KATHERINE G. FERRO

My brothers and I accompanied our parents on their journey of aging after they were hit by the perfect storm of Mom's physical decline colliding with Dad's mental diminishment, ultimately diagnosed as Alzheimer's. The situation was further fueled by 60 years of set daily life routines. From our perspective, they were no longer safe living in their large house in the town where we grew up, but no longer lived. From their perspective, they were fine. They had no desire to leave their comfortable home and all that was familiar.

For 5 years, we gently prodded, engaged in subterfuge, told small lies to get the end results we wanted. Mom and Dad finally moved to an apartment in a senior living facility not far from my home and Dad eventually transitioned to an Alzheimer's care facility. Throughout this veritable dance, with my brothers and me each taking turns with the lead, we would occasionally question our tactics or motives. We would then remind ourselves that all our actions were rooted in love for our parents and our desire to keep them safe. No regrets.

Alas, I could not keep regrets at bay following the final stage of the journey with my parents — the end of life. As a means of coping or perhaps of granting myself some grace, I have been able to differentiate between two types of regrets.

I found that low-impact ones are manageable. Those regrets sprang from situations I could not control. I regret that I was not able to go out to lunch, to the symphony, or to the cabin with Mom once we moved Dad to the Alzheimer care facility. As soon as Dad was moved, COVID hit and everything shut down. Mom died before the world opened up again. These are "it-would-have-been-nice" regrets.

"What-if" regrets are more difficult. They are the result of decisions that I made. They take up a lot of real estate in my heart and mind. I find it is best to repress them, but they rise to the surface nonetheless.

What if I had insisted that I see Dad after he was hospitalized with pneumonia? COVID rules said no visitors. Would pushing the staff have resulted in an exception? If I had been able to visit him, would it have made a difference to him? It would have made a difference to me.

After Dad's pneumonia was medically under control, the hospital social worker asked if Dad could receive hospice care in my home. What if I had been willing to forgo our usual Christmas traditions? Could we have modified our home to make it safe for Dad and still livable for us? Would it have made a difference to him? It would have made a difference to me.

What if I had adopted the attitude that I could walk into his room at the rehabilitation center despite COVID protocols? If I had just shown up in Dad's room, would it have made a difference to him? It would have made a difference to me.

What if I had been less sympathetic about staff shortages? What if I said that the holiday season was no excuse for poor service?

What if I demanded that the staff take my phone calls and answer my questions about Dad's status? Could I have seen Dad one more time before he lapsed into unconsciousness? When someone finally answered my phone call late in the afternoon of January 1, 2021, I was told to come right in. When I got there, the staff told me Dad was still alive, just breathing very shallowly. What if he wasn't? And what difference did it make?

I will always regret not having that one more chance to hear Dad chuckle, to see the sparkle that would still occasionally appear in his eyes. Yet I'll never know if I would have been blessed with either of those even if I had followed through with the "what-ifs."

## 25

# My Mother's Garden

## D'Arcy McKillop Farlow

In the early summer mornings, I like to sit in my small city garden as the sun slowly rises from behind the trees. This is the green moment of the day, when the light casts filigree patterns through the leaves. The hum of the city is muted, whereas the birds are lively and vocal. The colors emerge in the dawn light just for me, as I seem to be the only one of my neighbors sitting outside in my pajamas, with a coffee in hand.

I am often away much of the summer, and by the end of August, this is a sad, neglected garden, with many blooms lost to the heat and drought. While I'm here, I shower it with love and attention by watering, cleaning, and providing trims. Some plants and shrubs need a gentle haircut, while others require a vigorous re-styling. All gardens, no matter how tiny and compact, respond to this care. It could be a glorious place, if I were in the city more often.

My mother's gardens, in comparison, were beautiful, especially the garden in the shady backyard. Somehow, there were enough sunlit hours that she managed to coax vivid blooms from peonies, roses, Shasta daisies, and coreopsis, which flared in the shadows of the majestic beeches and maples. When my husband and I bought our first house, I asked my mother for cuttings from her garden.

She gave me some iris and a handful of promiscuous poppies that spread across the front of our first home, and then our next place. I occasionally drive by those former homes, and her poppies are still thriving. How did I forget to gather up a bunch for this garden?

I have a picture of my daughter, when she was two, standing in her pink sundress against the deep, fuchsia hues of the peonies in my mother's garden. Whenever I look at that picture, I am transported back to that exact June day. I was eight months pregnant, with life coursing through me, and filled with anticipation for the future, while appreciating the lovely afternoon. I sat under the trees with my mother, and we engaged in an easy-flowing conversation, until our talk took a sudden turn, as she expressed her regrets and sorrows.

"You know, I married the wrong man and have been unhappy with him most of my adult life. He has never shared my interests, or respected my views on the world, and I often feel unfulfilled by this relationship. My father begged me not to marry him."

I wasn't completely shocked by this; as kids, we sensed our parents were mismatched. My mother was rational and intellectual; our father was gregarious and emotional. But what was I to do with this information? Although I experienced compassion for her, we were at different stages in our lives, and I struggled to understand her midlife angst, feeling almost resentful that she would bring this jarring note into our afternoon. Today, if only it were possible, we would have a rich conversation that would be much more balanced and wise; two older women sharing their learnings from life.

Years later, when my mother was dying at home, I spent several months with her. In those final weeks of her life, we grew very close and found the courage to talk about her imminent death.

"What do you think will happen when you die?"

"Oh, I believe I will convert to pure energy and become part of the cosmos."

"Hmmm. Will you try to send me a message?"

"Perhaps you will recognize me in something energetic," she responded, with a smile.

We were together in her bedroom, when she conveyed her longing to have one last spring in her garden. That March, a remarkable thing happened. Spring came early, with unseasonably warm temperatures and a sudden blossoming of flowers and apple buds. I went for walk, in her beloved ravine behind her house, and came back filled with the exhilaration of spring.

"Mom, please let me help you outdoors, just to sit in this gorgeous sun for an hour. You can visit your garden."

"No, it is too late. I simply can't do this anymore."


My mother died five days later on a chilly March day. It turned out to be a false and exceedingly cruel spring. Those glorious magnolia blossoms, across the street, were blackened, and the apple orchards failed to produce a crop that year. The sharp blue skies, and frigid temperatures, enhanced my grief with a piercing sense of alienation. I wondered if I would ever enjoy spring again.

The sun has now emerged from behind the trees, and the day will soon be kicking into action. But this early morning time—in the cool of the garden, with thoughts of my mother—will sustain me for many hours. Standing up to go inside and start my day, a sudden noise makes me look up into the sky and I laugh out loud because there, above the trees, is a hot air balloon, full of energy.

# 26

## Little Scares, Immigration, and Inclusion

Nancy Avery Dafoe

"Could I have a cup of cider for my tata and abuela, too?"

On Halloween night, October 31, 2024, we served about 300 cups of cold apple cider to strangers who streamed onto my daughter's lawn in Silver Spring, Maryland. My husband passed out hot apple cider, mostly to the adults. Working as quickly as I could and tipping an awkward and heavy thermal jug, I did occasionally look up to find many families of recent immigrants. Mothers and fathers were still struggling with their command of English, relying on their children to ask a question. It was very dark that Halloween with an overcast sky and few lights on the suburban Maryland street, but a steady stream of kids and grownups arrived to see the haunted backyard my daughters, son- in-law, and grandsons created to entertain their neighbors.

The community my daughters and their families live in is a diverse one, a region just outside D.C. where working people strive to make the best futures for their children.

"Everybody is welcome," said my older daughter to the growing crowd as we started the evening adventures.

For the last few years, my two daughters, one of their husbands, and all four of my young grandsons have made elaborate preparations for their "haunted backyard," a free event for their community. They have collected cool fright items and hand-crafted scares, at their own expense, in anticipation of hosting this neighborhood experience. My other son-in-law baked macaroni and cheese brains to put into skeleton skull serving dishes and made meatloaf, bloody monster feet. My older daughter's in-laws and their daughter handed out a stores' worth of candy to the young ones as the line to visit the haunted backyard grew ever longer.

This past Halloween, my younger daughter added to the collection by making four larger- than-life-size dementors, based on the wraithlike creatures from the Harry Potter books and movies. Her process was intricate with amazing results, eliciting yelps from teens who ventured into the haunted yard.

A family affair, two of my nephews—my sister's sons who moved to Washington, D.C. recently—served as guides through the maze, taking one small group at a time. One son-in-law donned a realistic Pennywise mask to jump out at the older kids as they passed, wresting wild giggling or screams and more than a few flights down the path.

We served cider to a fair number of recent immigrant families in the lines. Immigration is such a fraught topic in this country right now, due in large part to many people's misperceptions about recent immigrants (since we are all immigrants at some point in our genetic ancestry). One aspect struck us, however, as we listened to the people: how much everyone cared for their children. Moms and Dads holding their little ones' hands, elderly grandparents present to protect and on hand to help. One father and his daughter collected cups that had fallen on the lawn and brought them over to put in the recycling bin. They were all quite wonderful. Everyone was exceedingly polite, grateful, and patient, considering the lines were very long, both for the cider and the haunted yard tour.

By the end of the long evening, my family gathered to clean up, laugh, and talk about another successful haunted backyard experience. None of us ever expected the event would grow to its current size. Everyone's brows were marked with sweat, an indication of how hard we had worked to make the haunting fun for all. After eating some macaroni brains and monster meatloaf, my nephews headed out because they had to get to their new jobs early the next morning. My four grandsons talked excitedly about their favorite reactions of the evening, especially the ones where they "got" their good friends from school. "Did you see him jump?" We noted all the visitors left smiling, laughing, or saying something along the lines of, "Can you believe it? They do this every year!"

Post haunted tours, my two daughters and one son-in-law discussed placement of the exhibits in the yard and whether or not some should be moved next year (yes, I agreed, the marvelous dementors need to be situated in the front). My other son-in-law was busy cleaning the kitchen. We were all tired but had a sense of accomplishment. That night, over 400 people came and visited my daughter's haunted yard, talked in hushed voices, took a step back in slight fright, and hugged their kids tighter. Grandparents were amazed and inspired. What a gift my daughters and their spouses have given to their community.

Immigrants have given back to this country every day—running the length and breadth of work from invaluable service and food industries to agriculture to winning Nobel Prizes in the United States. In 2021, three of the four Americans who won Nobel Prizes were immigrants. We are a land of immigrants when we stop to recognize the waves of people from other lands throughout our history.

I met a woman the day I started writing this essay. We talked while a group toured her specialty printing business. She is also a bookbinder and artist. Discussing her processes, she shifted the conversation to recognizing the contributions of her brother, a well-known graphic novelist, and her sister, a poet and college professor—all immigrants to this country from south of the border. They pay taxes and make invaluable contributions to our culture. Although meeting this bookbinder/printer/artist by chance, I know there are countless immigrants who make these beautiful contributions, making America wealthy in her people.

Before participating in my daughters' haunted backyard happening, I had never viewed this late Fall, costumed event in such a positive light. Many people would have fretted about crowd control upon seeing the huge gathering. But there was a heart-warming generosity of spirit all around in the haunted yard experience as new generations come to make America their home.

At the end of that night, a feeling of great peace and joy passed over us. While that feeling of loving inclusion has and will continue to find great challenges ahead, it was a night we would never forget.

# 27

## PA AND GRANDMA'S HOUSE

ANDREA CIFONELLI

Mom drives us to the Cicero post office where we meet Pa and Grandma Rizzo, a halfway spot between our houses. Whenever we meet at the post office, it means Danny and I are staying overnight at Pa and Grandma's. I see the white Audi when we pull into the lot. Grandma stays in the car, and Pa is waving his arms, directing Mom to park beside them.

I enjoy our time at their house, despite feeling slightly scared. Last time, I found myself alone in Aunt Claudia's childhood bedroom. I was admiring a pink and teal wristwatch wall clock beside her white wicker vanity when I heard a creaking noise that seemed to come from within the walls. I was startled and rushed to find Grandma. She brushed it off as "old house noises," but I remain unconvinced.

Pa and Grandma live in a Victorian house on Main Street in the heart of Oneida. The house is a village landmark with its Grecian pillars, scrolling cream molding, and pale-yellow siding. It served as the childhood home for multiple Rizzo generations. When I walk through the vestibule entrance from behind the house where the driveway ends, scents of sweet tomato sauce with sautéed garlic fill my nostrils. Grandma plants a soft kiss on my forehead, and Pa gives me a hug, squeezing me until my feet lift slightly from the cold entryway flooring. He swings me into the house, where I land on warmer ground. A draft of hot kitchen air quickly thaws my extremities, but a nagging chill lingers at the nape of my neck as I speculate about spirits in the walls. Pa takes our coats and, at my left, I hear bubbling from a vat of boiling pasta water in the kitchen and the murmur of Grandma's soap operas from the TV room ahead.

My imagination soars as I wander before dinner, pretending I'm a lonely princess trapped in a castle. I touch the textured wallpaper and shuffle aimlessly throughout red carpeted rooms. Lights dance along the dim hallways by sun passing through crystal chandeliers and ornate lamp shades with glass prisms dangling from the rim. If a piece of furniture isn't entirely velvet, there is at least one velvety part. I land on a tufted couch and study brush strokes on a painting of an old man with a child on his lap. Pa says it's our portrait, even though the grandpa has a beard and the girl has curly, blonde hair. A springer spaniel rests at their feet. A brass light installed in the frame illuminates their smiling faces.

The fireplace room with the stuffed songbirds is where we gather after elaborate holiday meals. The other fireplace room with the baby grand piano is where the Christmas tree is displayed in December. In the corner opposite the piano, towers of boxes wrapped in the sturdy gold paper from Pa's store spill from underneath the tree into the center of the room. Danny and I sit on the floor, ripping through most of the gifts.

Whenever I catch Pa in the Christmas tree room, he plops me onto the piano bench and places my thumb and pinky finger on two notes five keys apart. He reminds me how to teeter back and forth on the notes to accompany the melody that he plays. It's our special duet, and Grandma thinks it's a spectacular performance. A spot of burnt carpet behind the piano bench begs me to ask Pa about it every time. When I do, Pa jumps to recite the story about 12-year-old Uncle Joey burning the carpet when he was a kid. I pretend I've never heard the story before. If all the aunts and uncles are around, they chime in with more tales of mischief and mayhem. I feel envious of their childhood.

Two staircases lead to the second floor, but I never take the back one. It leads to the creepy part of the upstairs that has an abandoned second kitchen and a dusty dollhouse with cobwebs stretching the facade. A narrow hallway connects to Aunt Claudia's bedroom, where I heard the haunting wall noises. A grandfather clock lives on the landing of the main staircase, facing the front double-door entrance. It rings every hour, which is one of the other scary parts of Pa and Grandma's house.

There's also a third creaky staircase leading to an attic. One time, Pa and I sorted through a keepsake box of Mom's elementary school projects. I was on alert, scanning the attic for ghostly figures while sifting through the worn, plastic keepsake box. With a skeptical gaze upon the shadows ahead, my sorting hand grabbed a rigid, dead bird that had been wedged between Mom's treasured grade school triumphs. I resigned, then and there, from organizing dusty boxes in creepy attics.

Pa tells me that his own mother, my Great Grandma Tripoli, bought this big, yellow house all on her own in 1939. He says that she was ahead of her time, a single mother of four boys, and a business owner. Great Grandma Tripoli took occasional trips via boat to her home country of Italy. Her diaries indicate that she was depressed about missing her children but confident that teenage Pa could take care of everyone while she was away. She returned with Italian lamps and chandeliers, and all kinds of furniture and drapery to add to the big, yellow house. When Great Grandma Tripoli grew too old to live in a giant house alone, Pa proposed she live in his smaller house and essentially switch homes. She agreed and Pa moved his family, including my mom and her siblings, into the Main Street house.

My favorite piece to gawk at is the wall tapestry with the naked ladies lying under trees eating grapes. There are animals, fruit trees, and mystical creatures. Something new is revealed every time I study it. As I wander, I have regular visits with my other favorites around the house. I spend time with the porcelain ballerina putting on her pointe shoes. She sits on Grandma's dresser and gazes down at her feet. I imagine her turning her head towards me and complaining about her terrible foot pain and how the pressures of the ballet have become too much to bear. Her face is long and strained. Her body is slender as she bends to tie the tall laces up past her ankle. I check on the cranberry vase with bubbles suspended between layers of glass in the foyer and the scientific butterfly display in Pa's bedroom. His bathroom, with the clawfoot tub, has an old-fashioned telephone with a separate mouthpiece next to the toilet. I pretend to make important calls on all of Pa and Grandma's house phones. I dial by putting my finger in the hole of each number, moving the dial to a stop, removing my finger and watching with delight as it swirls back to center.

There are pretend house phones, too. When we get to Pa and Grandma's, Danny and I pull the toy bag out from the closet in the TV room. It's filled with old toys we've outgrown, but Grandma thinks we still like them. She also thinks I hate the taste of coconut, just like her. I don't have the heart to tell her that my taste buds have matured, and I like coconut now. The room smells like diapers and plastic when we pour the old Fisher Price toys onto the floor.

Unlike me, Danny doesn't waste precious time pretending to enjoy the old, stinky toys. He does his due diligence of dragging them out from the closet, then runs upstairs to Grandma's bedroom. He trots around in her dyed high-heeled shoes, clips on her earrings, and sifts through bedazzled sweaters. No one bothers him up there. We do our own exploring when we're at Pa and Grandma's. But I stay a while and pretend I miss playing with the toys until a smile of satisfaction appears on Grandma's face. She squeezes my cheek and says "Oooooo my little pooper dooper," which indicates that she'll leave me be. When she's left the room to tend to the pots on the stove, I abandon the toys and embark on an imaginative adventure of my own.

"Danny! Andrea! Your programs start at seven, it's T.G.I.F! Wash up and get your pajamas on."

Grandma is always on point with the TV shows. She calls them programs and likes watching them with us. No other adult takes interest in our shows. T.G.I.F is a series of sitcoms aired on Friday nights (Thank God It's Friday). My favorite show is Sister, Sister. Grandma has us wash our faces after we brush our teeth, which Mom never makes us do. I don't understand why I have to wash my face because it doesn't seem dirty. I run up to Grandma's pink-tiled bathroom when I hear that our shows are about to start.

"Danny! T.G.I.F. soon!"

He kicks off the heels. We're washing and brushing and, in a flash, we're back in the TV room with the scattered baby toys ready for our shows.

I sleep in Grandma's bed with her next to me. She keeps her bedroom TV on, and I'm thankful for the light because the house is scarier at night. I fall asleep staring deeply ahead at the paisley wallpaper. I memorize the pattern and try not to look around because

I don't want to see a ghost. Sometimes I look towards the door to check for lurking demons. Danny sleeps in Uncle Joey and Uncle Gary's room, where there are two twin beds and a gumball machine. They don't live here anymore. Danny is so brave sleeping alone in this house. I need Grandma and the TV light, and the wallpaper.

In the morning, Pa dances around the kitchen as he whips up breakfast. He sings a tune about what he's making.

"Creeeeeeeam of Wheat,

is so goooooooood to eat

you can eeeeeeeeeat it eeeev'ry daaaaay!"

Danny giggles as he watches Pa sing and dance. He kneels backwards on a chair. Grandma waves her hand, as if shooing a fly, and demands Danny sit before falling and tearing a hole in the cane backing as Mom did when she was a kid. Pa adds, "We can fix your head, but not my furniture!

Pa is a masterful cook, but he makes simple delights just for Danny and me, like Cream of Wheat. He tops it with butter and maple syrup. I get a ball of the hot cereal on my spoon, and I crush it at the top of my mouth. The chunks are the best.

Grandma is folding laundry on the kitchen table. Pa will leave for the store soon. I feel good about another visit to Pa and Grandma's without a ghost encounter. I don't want the resident spirits to ruin my happy times here. Danny doesn't seem to have a care in the world when he's here. It's a reprieve for both of us, and I wonder where his imagination takes him when he's in the big, yellow house.

# 28

## LAST GOOD DEED

### TRACY CHAMBERLAIN HIGGINBOTHAM

When I visited my boyfriend one winter weekend, I asked if I could borrow his car to drive home to my parents' house for the day while he worked. As he handed me his keys, he said, "Be careful, it is snowy outside and you are leaving early in the morning, so the roads might be slippery." Little did he know, the icy roads weren't what I had to worry about.

Halfway home on a back road, the car started stalling. Luckily, I pulled it off the road where it completely died. At 7 AM on a Saturday, there weren't cars going by and cell phones hadn't been invented yet. I was a 21-year-old girl stranded in 30-degree weather. I knew home was too far to walk in such freezing conditions. My options were very limited.

About 15 minutes later, a man in a pickup truck stopped behind my car. He asked if he could help and asked me where I was going. I told him, "Rome, where my family lives."

He said, "I'm going that way, I can drop you off."

With no other options in sight and a keen sense of feeling this man was okay, I accepted his offer. As I got in the cab of his truck, he moved a helmet over next to him telling me he was on his way to skydive.

As promised, this man dropped me off safely at my grandparents' house, where my uncle, a doctor, my aunt, and cousins lived. I told them my story. They were grateful I was safe, and the man didn't harm me. I knew in my gut he was okay, or I wouldn't have accepted his offer.

The following day, when I revisited my grandparents' house, my cousin asked me with concern, "Did you say the man who dropped you off was going skydiving?"

I replied, "Yes, why?"

"Well, Dad told me this morning one of his patients died skydiving yesterday. It must have been the man who gave you a ride here."

I was shocked. I later thought I was that man's last good deed on earth.

After finding out he was married, I asked my uncle for his address. I wrote a letter to his family telling them about the selfless act their husband and father did before he went skydiving. I felt they needed to know his act of kindness. I didn't get a reply, not that I expected one, but to this day, when I help someone else, I wonder, "Could this be my last good deed on earth?"

Life presents everyone with opportunities to assist other people in simple and complex ways. I believe strongly in opening a door for someone, taking the hand of an elderly person walking in the winter, or helping a person in church put on their jacket if it's stuck. These are good deeds. Expecting gratitude afterwards is not necessary because my heart is warmed by doing the act.

Sometimes I reflect on the skydiver's last act, I feel blessed I was able to be at the right place at the right time to offer him one more opportunity to do good on earth. Maybe you will be that person next time someone helps you.

# 29

## Ko Wai Au? Who Am I?

Hayley Marama Cavino

Ko Aorangi, ko Kopukairoa ngā maunga
Ko Moawhango, ko Waitao ngā awa
Ko Takitimu, ko Mātaatua ngā waka
Ko Mōkai Pātea te rohe pōtae
Ko Ngāti Whitikaupeka, ko Ngāti Whatumāmoa, ko Ngāti Pūkenga ki Tauranga ngā iwi
Ko Ngāti Whiti-tuturu te hapū
Ko Te Riu o Puanga, Ko Moawhango, ko Te Whetū o Te Rangi ngā marae
Ko Hayley ahau

> Aorangi and Kopukairoa are the mountains
> Moawhango and Waitao are the rivers
> Takitimu and Mātaatua are the ancestral canoes
> Mōkai Pātea is the home territory
> Ngāti Whitikaupeka, Ngāti Whatumāmoa and Ngāti Pūkenga are the tribes
> Te Riu o Puanga, Moawhango and Te Whetū o Te Rangi are the ancestral meeting houses
> I am Hayley

Growing up I wasn't aware of the above pepeha—a Māori form of introduction that also provides a history of my people for those "in the know." I was born in Taranaki—a place to which I have no known whakapapa, no genealogical connection. My mother was barely 19 when I arrived, less than two years after she escaped her abusive father. I grew up in the shadow of Parihaka—one of the pre-eminent sites of Māori resistance in Aotearoa/New Zealand—but I learned nothing about it in school. I learned nothing of our language.

I went to Bell Block Primary School in suburban New Plymouth until I was 12. Bell Block was named after the colonizer Francis Dillon Bell, but its real name is Puketapu, sacred hill. In the early 1970's nothing was as it truly was. I didn't know about raupatu, land confiscation, even though we were living at the heart of it all. In 1986 we moved to the South Waikato, also raupatu land, where I went to Putāruru High School. There, I asked to take Māori language as a high school student and was told no—I had tested too high for that. According to the school, Māori language was not meant for students who were deemed to be "academically inclined." Instead, I was told to take either French or German. It wasn't until university in the mid-90's that I would try again to learn our language in what was then the University of Waikato Māori Department—I cried after every class for reasons I couldn't understand and stopped going after the first month.

This is one story of my upbringing, but it is not the only story.

I have frequently represented myself with consideration of the absence of things, and in reference to what I am not.

I was not born on my land.

I was not raised in my Māoritanga.

I did not speak my language.

I was raised "away" by parents who were also away from their people.

As I've gotten older, this has changed. I remember differently now. I feel echoes and resonances. More recently I have been re-examining the content of my actual lived experience for tohu, signs, stories.

These stories are a terrain that matters.

These stories are still "us." These are still Māori stories.

Māori cultural traditions require that a speaker make themselves known to their audience. We reject the idea that narrators occupy an objective position—rather, our words are always subjective, reflecting our own pūrākau—our bloodlines, histories, stories, lived experiences—all the things that make up what academic scholars might call one's "social location."

I've shared a pepeha above. Part of what this does is authenticate me as a speaker—sharing a pepeha is a performance of identity and belonging where particular choices are made—certain genealogies are claimed while others are not. So, ko wai au? Who am I? The pepeha I provide here is only part of the story—both in terms of the whakapapa it leaves out and the ways it fails to reveal or address the complexity of the actual genealogies claimed—the richer "story within a story."

In this regard, I find that my pepeha needs annotation. Above, I have acknowledged the whānau of my maternal grandmother and grandfather, both of whom are Māori. My maternal grandfather's people come from Tauranga Moana; specifically, they are from Ngāti Pūkenga. Our stories in this locale indicate a degree of mobility pre-colonization, though with maintenance of distinct ties to the land in this resource-rich coastal area. Ngāti Pūkenga were one of the first iwi to have regular contact with settlers. We and other Tauranga Moana peoples were ultimately displaced in the second half of the 19th century through raupatu of upwards of 200,000 acres—almost all our collective territory. My grandfather was the first generation born "away" off iwi land.

My maternal grandmother is from Ngāti Whitikaupeka—she comes from the mountainous land-locked Mōkai Pātea region of the North Island's Central Plateau. Her people tell stories of ancestors coming over the mountain ranges after the great waka migration through the Pacific Ocean and "marrying in" to whānau that were already there. On our direct maternal line, we also have stories of ancestors emerging from the land through our female ancestor Haumoetahanga—there is no waka, no oceanic starting point. We have whenua whakapapa, the origin is land. My grandmother is also connected to Ngāti Whakaue (through her grandfather Henry Dargaville Bennett) and Rongowhakaata (through her father Iria-i-te-Rangi Halbert). On my maternal line, I am the first generation born off tribal lands.

At various points in my adult life, I have also claimed Ngati Porou, Ngāti Tūwharetoa, and Te Arawa belonging. The Ngāti Porou claim is inaccurate, as of this writing we have no known Ngāti Porou whakapapa. This claim originally came from my mother. She inherited small shares in Māori Land in the Gisborne area from her mother. She assumed Ngāti Porou belonging from this. This isn't surprising. Ngāti Porou is synonymous with Gisborne and the East Coast. Colonising has a flattening effect. Tribal maps were redrawn and relabeled by settlers, with only the largest tribal groups and most well-known names listed. Even now, neither Ngāti Pūkenga nor Ngāti Whitikaupeka, our two main tribal affiliations, appear on most contemporary maps delineating tribal territory. We are quite literally not on the map. The erasure continues. It wasn't until I was a doctoral student that Mum found out through Uncle Winston Halbert, her mother's younger brother, that the correct iwi is Rongowhakaata.

Our Ngāti Tūwharetoa belonging comes through Ngāti Whitikaupeka. Tūwharetoa is the larger tribal configuration that is the umbrella for many tribal groupings in the Central Plateau. As a result of my work in the last few years, I have become aware of a growing move to claim Mōkai Pātea as its own independent identity.

This is actually a reclamation, given that recent research affirms we understood ourselves as a separate tribal entity prior to colonization. The specificity of our Mōkai Pātea belonging makes political sense to me. It regrounds Haumoetahanga as a central and original female ancestor.

Te Arawa is the larger tribal grouping of which Ngāti Whakaue is a part. Our Ngāti Whakaue belonging is connected to H.D. Bennett, who married into our maternal line and came to Moawhango to live with Nanny Ngapera on her land. These changing claims simply mark our growing understanding of our history on these lands and the political savvy of our ancestors. It was often necessary to align with other nearby peoples, and to emphasize some genealogical connections over others, to resist and survive the insatiable thrust of colonization. For me, an important part of decolonization is re-introducing specificity and localized belonging from which we can then continue to enact this historical solidarity in the contemporary moment.

My father is an immigrant from Norwich, England, who came to Aotearoa/New Zealand in the 1960's as part of a Commonwealth resettlement program in the wake of his military service in the Korean War. My dad frequently espouses his "Englishness" but as an adult, I discovered his entire paternal line is Irish. There are clues as to the "why" of this, family stories and specificities beyond the known complex, fraught histories between England and Ireland. Stories within the story. It's a rabbit hole I've yet to fully engage. So far, I've traced as far back as our original Gaelic surname and the Dalcassians of the 3rd Century. There's a trip to Ireland planned for the Gregorian New Year.

Upon arriving in Aotearoa, my immigrant father harnessed the precarity of a childhood in which he experienced both the trauma of the Blitz and the relentless want of post-war austerity to become self-sufficient. Once here, Dad learned how to live off the whenua, awa, and moana. Land. Rivers. Ocean. He took me fishing before I could even walk. I grew up on Northern Taranaki beaches surf-casting and deep in the river valleys of Mōkau and Awakino fishing for trout and whitebait. I knew my way around a hand line and a fly-fishing rod before I reached double digits. In addition to practical skills, Dad taught me about balance, responsibility, and our relationship to the natural world. He modeled that we only take as much as we need. We leave the rest for someone else or for another day.

My parents used Mum's Department of Māori Affairs home loan to purchase a double suburban lot just outside of New Plymouth. On one section, Dad built our house, and on the other, my parents grew all the fruits and vegetables we ate and preserved. I distinctly remember them raising chickens on that double section, too. I'm still amazed at the audacity embedded in this refusal to live a typical suburban existence—we had a mini farm in the back yard. My parents shifted and forever altered how I understand what it means to live "in town."

Out the back of our place was reserve land. As kids, we spent countless barefoot summer days chasing the reserve creek down to the sea. The rocky black sand shore with its constantly evolving tidal pools was our playground. We spent long, hot days jumping from rock to rock; or alternately running, rolling, and leaping up and down massive sand dunes. We knew that little creek and its eventual ocean home as the ancestors they are. We knew the sway of the land. We knew complete freedom. As children, we were told by our parents to get out of the house and stay out. Be home by 8. I'd sometimes set my watch back and claim it must have stopped to buy additional time.

Genealogically, I come from raupatu land. When I consider the raupatu, I often think of the "big three"—Taranaki, Waikato, Tauranga. That's been my path too. I'm home now, in Tauranga. For the first time in my life, I live on my own whenua, on land to which I am intimately connected through the magic of whakapapa.

I was brought up with a tourist store taiaha propped up in the corner of the living room and fake Made in China "grass skirts" we dubiously trotted out when Dad's English relatives came to town. I was brought up by a brown mother who never spoke a lick of Māori but who, alongside my father, knew how to roll up her sleeves and put a kai on whenever some unexpected visitor or relative arrived.

I was brought up stopping by cousins' or aunties' homes on our way to anywhere we happened to be going. I was brought up knowing we belonged to something and someone else. We were still grounded and connected, however tenuously, to the root of what it means to be us.

# 30

## THE SPRINGBROOK

### DANIEL CALLAHAN

We were a restaurant family. My father had an unspoken rule that we were never to eat at fast food restaurants, so this was something we did rarely and only with our mother. It wasn't a matter of health consciousness, or even that (being a health inspector by trade) he had seen enough teenagers commit heinous acts of cross-contamination. My father believed fast food was a waste of money and that you could get better quality food by spending just a little more at a locally-owned establishment. We spent hours on road trips passing easily accessible golden arches to pull into a hole in the wall that just so happened to serve some of the best honey-dipped chicken I had ever tasted.

My parents also never shied away from bringing my older sisters and me to nicer, more "grown-up" restaurants. Even so, I knew that certain restaurants, the ones with menus printed on thick slices of soft paper attached to a hard folder and crisp linen tablecloths, were for special occasions. The Springbrook was our family's favorite.

I liked The Springbrook, but my favorite part about it was that it was located right next to a fish hatchery. If our reservation was an early one, and the weather was warm enough, my family would make the short walk from the Springbrook's parking lot across a narrow strip of lawn and up the paved driveway of the hatchery, where we were greeted by the quilted network of shallow cement pools. Some sections of the pools were covered by grates we could walk across to get a better look at the fish below. We all took turns putting on my mother's sunglasses to be able to see deeper into the water without the light reflecting off the water. The sunglasses, which I thought of as my "x-ray goggles," were too big for my head, so I had to hold them in place. No matter how many times I performed this magic trick, I was always surprised to see that they revealed the massive trout that had not been there a second ago but could now be clearly seen, swimming just below my feet. Some pools had only a select number of fish that gently glided through the water without a care in the world, while other pools were crammed with swarms of fish fighting for an extra sliver of space.

We were almost always the only ones there, and I always felt that my father was good at taking us to secret, fantastical places that no one else seemed to know about. It felt like we owned these spots.

The Springbrook was too crowded to seem like it was just ours, but it felt familiar and inviting no matter how much time had passed between visits. The restaurant itself was a white, two-story structure that looked like the clubhouse at an exclusive golf course. Outside, a green awning stretched across the driveway at the front door. Green-carpeted steps led to a calm, dimly-lit welcome area to the left of which was a dimly-lit bar with dark woods, capping off the country club feel of the place. The right side of the entryway opened to a series of thickly-carpeted dining rooms with pre-set table settings capped off with carefully-folded napkins.

I always imagined that the building had originally been a mini mansion that a rich family had lived in, and that the doorway near the hostess station was most likely once a sitting room when the family lived there. It now served as a large, open coat room. The same thick carpet from the dining rooms covered the floor, and a number of long windows looked out into the front drive of the restaurant to the left of the awning. If I placed my hands against the windows and pressed the side of my face against the cool glass, I could see the fence that separated the restaurants from the fish hatchery. Long silver coat racks had been installed along all of the walls of the room, and a variety of coats were jammed in like a clearance sale at JCPenney.

Even before I was old enough to start kindergarten, I knew to walk to our table with my hands at my side and not to talk at the top of my voice as I was often accustomed. I was a one-man parade of good manners. Older, white-haired patrons finished their early dinners, and the women often smiled down at me as my family passed through to our table, commenting on how well behaved I was or how dressed up I was if the occasion called for me to wear my clip-on tie. Once seated, some of these grandmotherly women continued to smile and wave at me. I was used to getting comments on my curly blonde hair from Mom's trips to the beauty salon.

"Look at those curls!" they would exclaim. "If I had those curls, I would never cut them!"

When the waitress came for our drink orders, my sisters and I would order Shirley Temples. My mom, who rarely drank, would ask for a Diet Coke, and my father would forgo his normal order of a beer for a martini with an extra olive. Before dinner came, we would share an order of Clams Casino. Once settled in, I could break character from "well-behaved boy" and make my parents laugh by placing the black olives from everyone's salad on the ends of my fingers, moving them around before eating them from my fingertips one by one.

The Springbrook would host our family's celebrations of Mothers Day, my parents' birthdays, and my sisters' confirmation. My friends and I would ride to The Springbrook in a limousine before the Junior Prom, and my class would gather in the back room for our 10-year high school reunion before getting drunk on the patio. But it was a less momentous occasion, just a late fall dinner when I was not even old enough for kindergarten, that would serve as my most memorable visit.

As my family was leaving the restaurant in a whirlwind of chatter and laughter, I watched my dad and sisters leave the restaurant through the heavy wooden door before I followed the back of my mother's legs into the coat room. Fall had arrived recently, but summer was still hanging around, so no one felt they needed a coat except my mother, who was always cold. She had worn her tan, full-length coat with the big buttons down one of the flaps. I watched my mother from behind as she crossed the room towards where she had hung her coat. The high of the night out had brought out my mischievous side, and I decided on an impromptu game of hide and seek. I ducked into the coats hanging on the opposite wall, finding the longest one and wrapping myself inside it. I could not help but giggling to myself and hoped my mother could not hear me from inside my cocoon.

I waited to hear her call my name.

I waited for the sound of her footsteps and, once I heard them, I planned to rush out from inside the coat with the loud roar of a monster.

I waited longer.

And longer.

I waited until it seemed like forever had passed. The heat from inside the stranger's coat I had hijacked made me feel flushed, and the material on the side of my face began to make my cheeks itch. This game was no longer fun. Abandoning my plan to scare my mother, I ducked out from the coatrack and found myself standing alone in the center of the coat room. My mother was nowhere in sight.

I immediately began to panic and ran to a window that overlooked the area under the green awning where I imagined my father and sisters were waiting for us after they left, but I only saw a black car pulling up.

No Dad.

No Courntey.

No Megan.

No Mom.

I turned and ran towards the open door of the coat room; I could see the hostess standing on the other side. Maybe she could help me. But, just as I got to the door frame, I saw the familiar camel-colored bottom of my mother's coat sweeping around from the side of the entryway. With all my might, I flung myself towards my mother's knees and wrapped my arms around her legs, happy to be reunited after what seemed like forever. I did not let go.

Even when I heard an unfamiliar cackling from above.

My arms still wrapped around the legs that suddenly felt too bony to be my mother's, I lifted my head and looked straight up.

A gray-haired, wrinkle-faced woman looked down at me with a wide grin and beady eyes.

"Well, that was a nice hug!" she cooed before letting out another fit of loud cackles.

I stepped back in sheer horror and burst into loud, wet tears.

I do not know how long it took my family to realize that none of them had escorted me to the car, but it must not have taken very long because, unbeknownst to me, my mother was watching this entire episode, hug and all, from the entryway to the bar, where she had just done a loop looking for me.

I did not see my mom because I was well into one of the most magnificent meltdowns of my childhood career. My whole body was as tense as a newborn's when first exposed to the elements. The combination of my mouth stretched open in a constant siren of screams and the tears pouring out caused my eyes to forcibly close. I did not even know it was my mother who was gently lifting me from the floor and into her arms. I only knew it was my mother when I heard her soft voice whispering into my ear.

"It's ok, it's ok. I'm right here," my mother repeated in a soft, soothing voice.

My screams stopped and the sound of my crying lessened only because it was now muffled into the shoulder of my mother's coat, but even my crying soon slowed once the safety of my mother's arms sank in.

My mother's imposter appeared at our side, having deposited her coat in the coat room.

"How about another hug?" she asked with a chuckle.

I only whimpered in response and flipped my head against my mother's hard shoulder to face away from the woman.

"I think he's all out of hugs tonight," my mom replied with a sweetness to her voice, apologizing for my response.

"Except for Mom," the woman said as she ruffled the curls on my head. "Except for Mom. There's always enough hugs for Mom."

As my mother carried me out of the restaurant, waiting at the door for a party coming in, I watched over her shoulder as the woman slowly shuffled over to her dining group. They all laughed, and one of the other women commented on my unintended hug. The woman waved goodbye in one more attempt to gain my trust. I could feel my dry tears on my cheeks as I watched her smile, but I did not smile back.

On the ride home, I sat sandwiched tightly between my parents in the front seat of the car. Everyone laughed as my mother told my father and sisters about me hugging the stranger, but I just leaned my head against my mother's side and enjoyed the softness of the familiar coat on the side of my face.

# 31

# MOONBLIND (AN EXCERPT)

## DEBORAH YOUNG BRADSHAW

To the west of the gray clapboard house lay a small orchard. The trees were neglected so dead branches cut awkward silhouettes against the sky. Despite neglect, some of the trees hung heavy with early fruit. In the middle of the orchard stood an old horse. He was still, except for his ears twitching flies away and a white tail that rose and flicked to the same purpose. The heavy arch of his neck and his muscular hindquarters bore witness to his working days, though they were long past. His coat was matted and burred around four heavy, yellowed hooves that curved up like long toenails on an old man unable or unwilling to reach his feet. His left rear foot was massive, much larger than the other three. He was born this way. It hadn't seemed to bother him much. He had been able to draw the plow and the thresher along with his working partner, Jerry, without difficulty, though the ungainly hoof required an extra-large shoe. His chest was deep and withers staunch, but ribs were visible under the flicking gray coat. He rested his tapered nose in a crotch of one of the apple trees. Sparrows swooped and sang from limb to limb around him, one resting on his back briefly. He gave it no notice and only flicked his tail wearily at the horseflies.

Two boys worked busily in their mother's vegetable garden behind the house. The younger, Bobby, crowed each time he found a ripe tomato and ran to show his older brother, John.

"Yeah, Bob, that's a beauty. Don't throw it into the basket, now. You got to put 'em down gentle or they'll bruise."

"Ok, John. I will. How many did you get?"

"Oh, about 20 so far."

"Aw, I only got 6."

"That's alright, buddy. I'm bigger than you."

They worked quietly for a while. The sun began to drop, and a chill came up. Their mother, Erma, leaned out the back door and called.

"That's enough for now, boys. It's getting damp. Please bring the tomatoes here and then go help your father feed calves."

The boys picked up the basket and turned toward the house.

"Johnny, let's see Tom before we go to the barn. We gotta fill his water bucket."

They set the basket on the back porch, then skirted the house and trotted toward the orchard. They slid, one after the other, under the lowest barbed wire. Old Tom's ears swiveled toward the boys working their way through the tall grass toward his tree. John checked Tom's water trough and found it dry.

"Oh, jeez. We forgot to water him yesterday, poor fella. We can fill it from the creek. There should be enough water. It rained earlier in the week."

Tom's feed bucket, a galvanized tub with rough, rope handles, was empty too.

"Hey, boy! How ya doin'?"

John reached up and ran his hand along the creature's burly neck. The long mane was tangled and yellow with age. Tom lifted his nose out of the tree crotch, nickered, and swung his head down to greet the boys. Bobby scratched the horse's nose. Tom's eyes were white at the center, milky like stars and ringed by navy blue like the night sky. John could see fine red blood vessels creeping in from the whites of the eyes, over the cornea. Tom nickered again and bobbed his head slightly. Bobby squatted to the ground, found a red apple, stood and held it in his palm to the horse's mouth. Tom sniffed and huffed, his damp breath warming Bobby's palm. The creature accepted the fruit with warm, supple lips. A hollow crunching told them Tom relished the treat and sweet bits of apple dropped from his mouth.

"Dad says Tom is Moonblind."

"How come? What happened? Did he stare at the moon too long?" asked Bobby. John shrugged his shoulders.

"Naw, it's just a saying. I dunno, he's old."

"What are we gonna do with him? He can't just stay out here all winter."

"I know it. Guess we'll bring him in the barn. Dad says we oughta sell him 'cause he can't work anymore and he's blind, an' all. He's been sayin' that for a long time."

"I hope he don't sell Tom."

"Me neither. We can take care of him. You're a good ol' boy, huh Tom?"

"Dad says we won't have enough hay for the cows this winter. Will we have enough for Tom?"

"Prob'ly not."

John scuffed the hard earth with one boot and felt something rise in his throat. John grabbed the watering pail that hung on a nail on Tom's tree, and the boys ran deeper into the orchard. A small stream had gouged the earth into a deep gully and, at its base, ran clear water in several rivulets. John laid the pail on its side and held its lip under water. As the pail filled, John's eyes explored the steep hillside of the horse pasture dotted with shrubs. He felt an ache in his chest, something between pain and happiness, and it nearly stopped his breath. He and Betty used to play there among the trees. She was the teacher, and John was her obedient student. It was easy to mind her. She was kind and strong, like their mother.

*Before the sickness, Betty was stronger than me. She knew things. Like when Mother was sad or when we were in trouble with Dad. She was small and pale, but it was like her pallor overcame me, left me weak and uncertain, looking to her for what I should do or say next. She had straight brown hair. It shone. Her bangs were blunt, honest, and caught me out whenever I tried to pass a half-truth or a trick on her. The steady gray eyes on me were like God watching. I was her help, her hand, her second, her lieutenant. Every action I took was meant to please her. All I needed was to see those gray eyes soften, to watch for the slight upturn of her mouth. Then I could rest for a while. I could rest in her kindness. And then the sickness came, and she was gone.*

The next afternoon, an orange school bus nosed west on Route 13 and stopped in front of the house. Tom lifted his head and pricked his ears. John flew off the lowest step of the school bus and didn't stop until he reached his mother's kitchen. His sister and brother followed close behind. Their mother, Erma, was at the sink scalding tomatoes.

"Careful, kids. This water's hot." The children's baby sister, Patricia, all dark brown curls and brown eyes, got up from the floor and toddled toward the other children. She wrapped her arms around two legs, squeezed, and shrieked with delight.

"Hi, Mom. What's to eat?"

"There's bread and butter on the counter and I think there's still some applesauce in the icebox. Don't eat too much or you'll spoil your supper. Kathy, you cut Bobby and Pat a slice of bread, please."

Erma counted to 30 seconds under her breath, watching for the tomato skins to split. Then she poured off the water and began to slide the skins off the tomatoes. She filled the kettle with water again and set it back over the flame. Wooden chairs scraped the floor as the children readied the kitchen table to eat. Bobby laid out plates and then knives. Kathy went to the ice box, retrieved a bowl of glassy brown applesauce, and dipped some onto each plate. Patty threw herself over the seat of the chair and tried to hike a chubby knee up to gain her seat, but John scooped her up, seated her, then wrapped a towel around her neck like a scarf.

It was silent while the children ate. The kitchen felt warm and dark. Late afternoon sun streamed in the open west window, and the patterned curtains lifted on a breeze carrying a mix of scents from the orchard: damp earth, rotting apples, manure, and cut grass. As he ate, John noticed Tom out the window and felt a pang. He turned and ladled a spoonful of the cool, sweet applesauce into Patty's open mouth. He noticed the way her curls clung to her broad cheeks in the damp of the kitchen. Erma cored and sliced the tomatoes into wedges and slid them into a pot on the stove.

"How was school?" They all began to talk at once.

"One at a time, please."

"Mrs. Bushnell dyed her hair. It used to be the color of a mouse. Now it's the color of a blue mouse." The children tittered.

"John, there's no need to make fun of others, especially your teacher. What did you learn about today?"

"Well, we're still practicing long division and then we had a game where we split the class in two and answered history questions for a prize. Our team won by a lot. Some of the questions were easy, like who is the father of our nation? Some were hard, but I still got most of them right. Like, which of the 13 colonies was the first to ratify the Constitution?

"Delaware," said Kathy.

"Yep. I like history the best, especially about the early days. Mr. Swingruber, he's reading from a big book called 'The Deerslayer.' It's about a man with a long rifle, they call him Hawkeye. He named his rifle 'Killdeer,' and he is the best shot ever. Mr. S. said the story takes place around this area, back when there were Indians and just a few white settlers. I want a long rifle and to go hunting with Dad. I think I'll be old enough this fall. Then, when Uncle Joe comes up from New Jersey next time, I can shoot woodchucks with him. Someday, I'll be a sniper like him, a really, really good shot."

"Me too," said Bobby, swinging his legs excitedly. His cheeks were bright and glossy.

"Alright now, please clear the table and take care of your dishes, and Kathy, run down to the cellar, and get me some potatoes for dinner. She turned to supervise the table clearing and, smiling, resumed her task at the sink. John sat watching his mother, postponing his trip to the barn. Strands of brown hair had escaped her bun and rested lightly on her face. She poured another kettle of boiling water over a bowl of knobby red tomatoes, and the wisps of her hair drifted upward in the rising heat. Her quiet gray eyes seemed far away, and John wondered what she was thinking about. Sadness tugged at him. He rose quickly and went to put his boots on.

The sun was still warm and autumn-bright when the boys headed across the road to the barn. Bobby took two steps for every one of

John's. A light wind from the west blew a few orange leaves across the yard. Beyond the barn, the hills across the valley rose into dense woods, a mix of evergreens and deciduous. The hardwoods tried on various autumn shades, the outermost leaves of the maples, burning orange, mustard, and scarlet, but summer green still dominated the hillside. A chevron of Canada geese cried together, circling low down near the river.

Walter Schmid looked up from his pail when the boys entered the barn. He was very tall and very lean, and he broke into a wan smile when he saw them. His thin brown hair was combed neatly to the side, and he was clean-shaven even so late in the afternoon. He poured a bucket of frothy milk through a soft white filter and into a milk can in the center aisle.

"Hey, boys. How was school today? Did you learn anything?"

"Naw, the usual stuff, Dad, except we learned about Hawkeye, Le Longue Carabine. That's what the Frenchies called him. He named his rifle 'Killdeer.' Do you think I'm old enough to hunt with you in November?" John said.

"Well, let's see. You'll be 8, is that right?"

"Yep, in April, but I'm grown up for my age. My teachers tell me that a lot."

"Well, your aim is pretty good. Maybe Sunday we can practice a little, but you can't go hunting 'til you're 16. That's a long way off. Now you better get busy with the calves, it's nearly 5 o'clock."

John could hear them bawling. The boys headed down the center aisle of the barn. On either side, rows of tails switched and arced. Suddenly, a bright yellow stream of pungent urine gushed in front of them. They veered out of the way and then turned toward the calf pen.

The calves jostled and bleated excitedly when they saw the boys. John and Bob each took a pail and went to the milk house. A tall milk can had been set aside for the calves. John tipped it, filling both pails. Thick yellow cream decanted first followed by foamy white milk. They returned to the pen where ten or more pink noses fought to get into the rich milk. The larger ones bunted their way forward and drank greedily. The boys refilled several times until all had drunk, and then they dipped grain from the granary, pouring a line of it in front of the pen where the calves could reach it by straining through the wooden slats. Finally, they spread loose hay for the older ones. The boys then turned their attention to cleaning and began to scrape the sweet-smelling yellow calf manure into piles, and from there, John forked it into a wheelbarrow, which he emptied into the horse-drawn spreader behind the barn.

"OK, Bud, time to scrape the alleys. I'll do that, and you can clear out the water buckets," Walter said.

Working in the aisle, John chatted with his father, who dipped between the cattle, moving slowly down the line. The milking machines huffed rhythmically, and their rubber hoses bounced in time. The hired man, Lenny, had nodded at the boys when they entered the barn. Now he worked steadily down the line in parallel with Walter, washing udders, applying the milkers, massaging the last of the milk from each quarter of the udder, and then pulling the machines off with a sharp sucking sound. John continued to talk about hunting, and then on to muskrat trapping in the brooks. Walter listened quietly, nodding here and there when a nod was called for.

After chores, the boys fed and watered Tom, then headed to the house to wash for supper. At dinner, the conversation skipped from subject to subject, concerning first school, then the farm, then the approaching winter.

"Dad, when are we going to bring Tom into the barn?"

"You raise a good point, son. I was thinking it's finally time to sell him. Otherwise, we'll have to keep him in hay and oats through another winter."

"Who'd buy ol Tom?" Bobby asked. Walter and Erma shared a glance.

"Well, you never know, son, what motivates people. Say, remember we've got supper at the church this Saturday. I told them we'd supply some milk and, Mother, aren't you making pies?"

"Yes, five pies, and I'll be needing you boys to pick some of the riper apples for me Saturday morning."

"Sure, Mom."

After dinner was cleared and the dishes done, John, Kathy, and Bobby sat at the kitchen table to do their homework. Walter retired to his chair in the living room, and Patty climbed into his lap to play. Erma continued her canning operation in the kitchen. By now, the tomatoes formed a rich puree on the stovetop. Erma seasoned it with garlic, salt, and basil leaves, covered the sauce to bring it to a final boil as she prepared the canning jars. Walter called to her from the living room.

"Mother, why not leave that 'til the morning. You've had a long day. It'll keep."

"Walter, the paraffin is melted and ready, and I've sterilized the jars. If I wait 'til morning, I'll have to do that all over again." Walter sighed, then stood up from his chair holding Patty in his arms. He carried her into the kitchen, kissed her, and set her on a chair at the table with the others. The kitchen was damp and warm, rich with the scent of tomato sauce. A hint of cooked cabbage lingered from dinner. Together, Erma and Walter worked at the canning. Walter poured the sauce from the heavy kettle into 48 glass jars, and Erma sealed each with liquid paraffin.

While John worked on long division, he could hear his mother speaking to his father near the stove in a quiet tone.

"Walter, the feed store called again today. I put them off, but it's getting harder. I told 'em you'd bring a check soon. They said they need it by the 15th."

John looked up at his father. He was a handsome man. Gray hairs mingled with brown, and the flesh of his eyebrows was beginning to droop. He had a long, straight nose that came to a decided point. Erma told her children it was a Swiss nose, refined and proud. John often grew impatient with his father's half-hearted approach to farming. John could see it and had heard his friends comment on how the whole place was sliding downhill. It seemed to John like Walter's mind was always somewhere else than on what he was doing.

Walter wasn't the same since Betty died. He always seemed sad and far away, as if he was always in the middle of something but forgot what he was doing. John thought about this often, and it made him angry. Walter wasn't the only one who missed Betty. She was everybody's favorite. She was John's favorite. She was an angel, so bright and so rare, she shone like a sun from a faraway place in the sky. John's heart ached whenever he thought of her. No, it wasn't only Walter who missed her.

# 32

## Time for Us

### April Bradley

I tried my first "cigarette" when I was around 10 years old. It wasn't a real cigarette, rather, it was the leaves from a teabag ripped open and wrapped in wide-ruled paper, freshly torn out of my best friend, Jill's, notebook. Jill's mom worked long hours as a bartender, which was good for us when we wanted to be mischievous and watch TV until late into the night, or smoke home-rolled tea while squatting in a corner of the kitchen. I coughed and gagged when the smoke burned my lungs but after a few puffs, I pretended I was experienced and held it between my fingers like I'd seen Jill's mom do countless times. By the time I was in high school, I was smoking real cigarettes a few days a week with girlfriends, mostly when we'd drive around with nowhere to go or while at field parties. These cigarettes, the occasional bowl full of weed, and a few beers were the extent of how I experimented with drugs and alcohol throughout my adolescence and into my young adulthood. It wasn't until I was 42 years old that I tried psilocybin mushrooms for the first time.

Much like my introduction into taboo, sometimes illegal, substances I tried mushrooms for the first time with my current best friend. But this time, she wasn't a pre-pubescent girl who loved to hoola-hoop and cartwheel in the yard with me, she was a physician and my dear friend of 25 years. My friend, Sadie, had learned of a place just north of New York City, where thousands of people have gone over the last 15 years to have an experience on hallucinogenics. It was advertised by word of mouth only, and set on a sprawling private property that sat on a hill. It had a garden that provided guests with home-grown tomatoes, peppers, beans, and their chickens provided our eggs in the morning. There was a beautiful backyard patio surrounded by tall, full trees that had delicate soft white lights strung throughout the canopy. It gave us the sense we were deep in the forest. This patio is where the "ceremony," our "journey," would take place. Those are the words the facilitators used, journey and ceremony.

We were emailed a packet of information and loose instructions to follow, such as eat a healthy, balanced diet free of ultra-processed foods, abstain from alcohol, sleep well, and exercise regularly the week leading up to the ceremony. On the day of the ceremony do not drink caffeine, have a protein-filled breakfast but do not eat after 12 PM. We later learned that having an empty stomach was one way the facilitators could somewhat control how long we would trip; we would all be coming down around the same time if the "plant medicine" didn't compete with food. The spread they prepared for us afterwards made it well worth the wait: fresh vegetables and fruits, homemade salsas and hummus dips, mixed nuts, various breads and pretzels, tuna fish, and multiple types of salads.

Sadie was more nervous than I was. I was excited and ready. I had followed their instructions to a fault and I felt both mentally and physically prepared. Sadie never liked giving up much control. She was worried that a significant trauma from her childhood would arise and she wouldn't know how she'd react. I wondered if there would be anything in the recesses of my brain that would rear its head. The facilitators interviewed each of us briefly, standard questions about types of medications we took regularly and if we had ever hallucinated on any mind-altering substances before. They explained and described how the entire night would go in an effort to quell any fears and help us feel like we were in control. Over the course of 5 hours, they would give us three separate doses of plants and explained to us what they were.

Neither Sadie nor I had any experience with drugs stronger than marijuana and were honest about that; we were the only two, of about 20 people present, who had never tripped before. We soon learned that there were only five of us who had never been to the property before, the rest were repeat customers. I supposed this spoke highly of their reputation and experience.

In the early evening, we all gathered in the front yard and were handed our first dose. We listened to the owner of the property wax poetic about himself, his wife, and how they have enjoyed running this business over the years. They were driven to provide for others what had worked so well for them in living through and surviving significant events, tragedies, and traumas in their lives. They told us of the shaman they used and trusted for the last 20 years. They encouraged us to walk through the garden, smelling and touching whatever we wanted before they led us to the back patio where our mats, pillows, and blankets awaited us. They instructed us to get comfortable and put our eye masks on. We were encouraged to keep our eye masks on so the journey was inward and experienced individually as opposed to having visual hallucinations of our surroundings. This was to be a solo experience with oneself despite the thirty other people present. They also warned that some of the more experienced attendees were taking stronger substances, similar to

Ayahuasca, so it was important that we didn't get distracted by their experiences or what they were doing. They gave one final instruction to keep our hands and words to ourselves, not to bother anyone else, and if we felt we needed to get up off our mats, to raise our hand so that one of the seven facilitators, who remained sober throughout the ceremony, could help us get up and walk with us. Then, around six o'clock in the evening, the facilitators gave us our second dose.

Before arriving to the retreat, Sadie and I decided we would not lay next to one another so we could not, or be tempted, to influence each other. I locked eyes with Sadie as we each received the plant medicine and raised my small cup in the air directed towards her, "Cheers." She smiled at me and did the same. We put the cup to our lips and took our second dose, which was tastily infused in chocolate. I waved and blew her a kiss before snuggling up with my father's oversized sweatshirt, its hood pulled far down over the top of my head, and my blanket pulled up to my chin. I pulled down my eye mask and breathed deeply for what felt like ages. In the beginning, I could feel myself panicking about what was to come, of how I may react. My heart was racing but I was in better control of those emotions than before. I let the panic come and then I easily let it go. I had never felt so in control of my worries. Throughout the experience, it was as if I was swiping away images or thoughts I didn't want to waste my time on. Before long I began to feel warm and a tingling sensation throughout my body. I touched my arms, shoulders and put my hand on my chest, because the rhythm of my heartbeat made me feel incredibly satisfied. I felt light, in control, and happy. I began to see some bright colors. But it wasn't long before those faded away and the most delightful, pleasant, happy images of my son, Oliver, appeared. This is why I was here, why I drove 4 hours and trusted a process I had no experience with, all so

I may spend some time and energy with Oliver. I smiled so much, I briefly wondered what I may look like to others: my hand on my heart and a broad, bright smile underneath the hood of sweatshirt and eye mask. There was no sense of time, it was warped, but it felt like I was smiling for hours.

As if I was a visitor looking in on the scene itself, I saw Oliver in my arms after I delivered him, watched myself stare at his perfect face, saw myself crying. I let myself see that image for a while and even cried while I thought about what a dark and difficult time that was, but I soon swiped it away. Next, I watched Oliver and my living child, our toddler, playing on the couch together laughing and sharing toys. After that, I was tying his bow tie as we stood in the front room of our home, and I was smiling up at him, an image of my 16-year-old son before his prom. I was so happy to spend the evening with Oliver in all the different ages and stages of life he will never experience; Oliver died just before his due date because I had developed severe preeclampsia.

There were some moments I spent with my father too, he had recently died 2 years earlier from Parkinson's disease. I enjoyed images of being six years old and climbing on his lap, sitting with him in his recliner chair as he watched the nightly news. I could feel his hairy chest on my cheek and smell the cool spring air and fresh cut grass on his shirt as I snuggled in, fitting perfectly under his arm.

As I began to come down from my trip, I stopped seeing such vivid images and memories. I clung to them as long as I could, but I began to become more aware of my surroundings. The consistent sound of crickets and the movement of other participants around me took over my sense of hearing. The music that had been playing over surround sound speakers was turned down slightly. I began to think about Sadie, hoping and wishing she was OK. A feeling of protection and love for her came over me and I sat up, pushed my eye mask up and looked over to where she was lying. She was still, under her blanket with her eye mask on. I looked around and saw that about half the participants were up and walking around. I was smiling but only realized it as I watched a facilitator walk gently over to me with a huge smile on her face. She knelt down and offered both of her hands to me, telling me I looked wonderful and happy.

"I feel so happy!" I whispered loudly to her, like it was a secret I was afraid to share.

She helped me to my feet and showed me to the kitchen, where I saw a mountain of food. I filled two plates and carefully made my way back out to Sadie, where she was now sitting up and looking around.

"Hi!" I whispered to her as I sat down next to her, unable to control my smile.

"Hi…"she said cautiously. I could see tears in her eyes.

"Oh no, are you OK? How was your experience? What happened?" I asked gently, worrying.

"I'm a good person" she responded as tears rolled down her cheeks. I'm a good person and I don't have to be perfect," she explained further.

"I know, I know you are!"

Through tears she explained that she had a hard time letting go of control but when she finally did, she saw her husband, their life, and their children. She saw how she tries to control aspects of her life, sometimes without meaning to, and that she realized she doesn't have to. That she is a good person who suffers from guilt and pressure. We hugged tightly and I told her that she never had to pretend or hide anything from me, I was her and she was me. She had let go of a lot of emotional baggage, she was light and more carefree than I had seen her in a long time. She was equally support-ive, wanting to hear about what I had seen and how I felt having spent so much time with images of Oliver and my dad. We spent the next hour picking at food, walking the grounds, and reveling in our individual experiences with one another. We were content and satisfied. Exhaustion took over and we moved out mats next to one another and finally fell asleep under the stars.

The experience wasn't joyful for everyone. The next morning, we sat together under the shade of the canopy, led by the facilitators through a 3-hour debrief. We heard stories of loneliness and fear. A few people talked around their unresolved issues with their parents. One young woman spoke about a lifetime of feeling abandoned, stemming from her mother's inability to care for her when she was young. One man no longer had meaning in his marriage. But even with the sadness of these stories, people were happier, lighter, and more content. There was a sense of community and belonging in the rituals we experienced together, and we were not alone. We were challenged, privileged really, to spend time with ourselves and our minds; for a few that was near impossible but for me it was pure joy to have uninterrupted time with my son and my father.

# 33

## ROUND TRIP

### ANN SUTERA BOTASH

"Ann, wake up," Mom whispered softly and waited. Like a distant hum, "Wake up, now," she repeated.

My mother's voice floated into the darkness. Was that really Mom, or just a dream? Then, I remembered, and sat straight up in bed. I had a plane to catch. Mom stepped back quickly into the dark bedroom that I shared with my sister.

"I'm up. I'm up," I assured myself as much as my mom.

"Shhhh. You'll wake your sister."

She disappeared down the hall as I pulled off the layers of blankets, including Grandma's ivory afghan, doubled over for extra weight and warmth. At 4 AM on the weekend before Thanksgiving in 1984, the heat was turned down for the night. I longed to crawl back under the covers and wait for the rumble of the metal pipes, echoing like a hammer throughout the baseboards and warming our house. Instead, I felt around blindly to find the back of the desk chair for my teal interview suit, white blouse, and pantyhose. I ran my fingers through my recent pixie cut and felt my dark brown hair sticking straight up. After pulling on my outfit and slipping into my black low-heeled pumps, I reached for the matching black leather bag on the floor at the foot of my bed.

That past summer, Mom and Adeline had driven me to New York Medical School in Westchester for my first interview. Adeline was my mother's older cousin. Having lived with Mom's family for most of her life, helping Grandma to raise Mom and her brothers, Adeline was like a second mother to Mom and now to me, my brother, and sister. While I interviewed for a few hours, Mom and Adeline shopped in the White Plains Mall. Adeline looked at me expectantly as she handed me a large shopping bag from Macy's.

"It was on sale," she said simply.

I peered into the bag and saw a large black purse with numerous pockets and zippers. It was something an older woman might carry. An old-lady purse. I thanked them and hoped I did not sound ungrateful. Despite my initial apprehension, the purse came in handy on my subsequent interviews.

That morning, I fished around on my desk in the dark, finding three quarters to drop into one of the zippered side pockets. I would have to remember to genuinely thank them.

Except for my hair, I was almost ready to go. I checked again to make sure my round-trip Delta airline tickets were in the old-lady purse and then scooted into the bathroom for a pit-stop and final hair smoothing. Down the hall, Dad was already dressed, drinking black coffee in the kitchen. Mom, wearing her pink nightgown, was holding out a slice of buttered toast for me.

"Mom, I don't think I can digest anything this early in the morning," I said. She tucked the toast into a plastic sandwich bag and slipped it into one of the inside zippered side pockets of my purse.

"Here, take this for lunch because you won't have time to get food before you come home." She tucked in another plastic bag. This one was peanut butter on bread. She was referring to my tight travel itinerary to fly round trip in one day to Washington, DC. The plan was that my dad and I would leave early, drive for two hours, and arrive at LaGuardia about an hour before the Delta shuttle. My flight would arrive in DC, about an hour and a half before my 10 o'clock interview at George Washington University (GW). We had timed the day perfectly. When the interview ended, I would fly back before nightfall. GW was one of the only med schools to offer a Saturday interview. It was a relief to not miss a day of college classes and Dad could drive me to the airport without having to take a day off from work. Yet, they only offered me the one day, with no other options.

Although my parents supported me throughout all my interviews, they were less enthusiastic about this one. GW had the most expensive tuition of all the medical schools to which I had applied. If it turned out to the be the only school offering me admission, the cost would be a barrier. Still, I thought I should at least see it for myself. Until one of the other schools offered an acceptance, I felt compelled not to miss an opportunity.

"Aren't you cold?" I asked my mother. There had already been a light snow earlier in the week.

"Yes," Mom said. "But I am going right back to bed, as soon as you leave."

"Let's go," Dad motioned toward the front door.

"Do you have quarters?" Mom asked.

"Yes, I took some from my desk."

I needed the quarters for that evening, for my return trip from LaGuardia. The flight would bring me back to LaGuardia and I would use one of the quarters at a payphone to call the Poughkeepsie Limousine service. The phone number was written on an index card in my purse. My parents had pre-paid the forty dollars for the one-way trip back from the airport. With the second quarter,

I would call my parents when I arrived back in Poughkeepsie. The drop-off was at The Red Roof, a local motel on Route 9. My dad called it The Red Roach, as a reminder that it was a bit seedy. I had some cash for the taxi to and from the airport in DC. The third quarter was for an emergency.

My dad took my dark beige trench coat out of the front closet and held it open.

"You've gotten a lot of use out of Martha," he noted.

"Yes," I said as I tied the coat-belt around my waist.

Martha was the name Dad dubbed my coat. He had named several of my coats. This custom began with a brown suede jacket that had a frontier-ish look to it that he named "Natty Bumppo." We had a bookshelf in the basement with James Fenimore Cooper's "The Leatherstocking Tales." Dad encouraged me to read them to learn about the American frontier. Martha was purchased and named later, when it became apparent that Natty Bumppo was not appropriate for every occasion. While I was a high school senior, my social studies teacher phoned to say a spot had opened at the last minute on the waiting list for the class bus trip to Washington, DC. With my parents' permission, I could go. My mother decided Natty Bumppo would have to stay home. On the day before that trip my mother and I made an essential purchase, a London Fog raincoat from Flah's department store. Ironically, Martha, whose full name was Martha Washington, was about to have another Washington-related adventure.

Mom wished me luck as Dad and I walked gingerly down the uneven shadowy sidewalk to the Chevy Malibu. This was the third big trip in the past few months for this car: New York Medical School in Westchester, then Buffalo, and now LaGuardia. I expected the ride to go smoothly, like the others. Dad turned up the heat and I fell asleep before we reached the Taconic Parkway.

I awoke to Dad muttering, "Dammit!" I could the see the water vapor from his breath reflecting off fading light from the dashboard. Despite the cool temperature, beads of sweat were on Dad's forehead.

Our headlights should have been shining brightly ahead into the 5:30 AM darkness on Interstate 684. Dad leaned over the steering wheel and gripped tighter as the way ahead became dimmer.

"We have to stop," he said. "Something's wrong, maybe the battery or a connection."

"Take the exit."

I pointed to Exit 10, Bedford, Mount Kisco. We had been on the road for an hour and the plane would be leaving in a little over two hours.

Dad pulled off the exit and into a gas station. Unbelievably, there was also an auto repair garage right next to the station. Unfortunately, at that early hour, it was closed.

He pulled into a parking spot, turned off the engine, and popped the hood. I peeked at the engine too, feeling the warmth against my face while having no idea what I was looking at. After a few minutes of fiddling under the hood, Dad went back to the driver's side and turned the key. Nothing happened. Not even a sound. He tried again. Nothing.

"Let's call your ma," Dad said as he nodded toward a telephone booth near the road. Dad never liked to carry change, so I reached into my old lady purse and located one of the quarters.

"Here," I said, nervously glancing at my watch. If Mom left immediately, she would arrive in an hour and I might still make it to the gate before take-off at 7:31 AM. Dad phoned her and said to take Exit 10, South, to NY 172.

"We are on the left-hand side of the road, at Al's Auto Shop." He added, "Big red sign, you can't miss it."

I shoved my hands into my coat pockets as we waited near the road, glad Mom had suggested I zip in Martha's wool lining. The road was quiet and empty. We paced in the parking lot to keep warm.

A little over an hour later, in the early light, my parent's Dodge Colt sped past.

"Here, here!" We waved our arms wildly. Mom was intently peering away from us, to her left. We were not on the left side of the road; we were on the right. That's when I snapped.

"Dad! What did you tell her?"

My voice cracked. I stared straight ahead, in the direction of our disappearing ride.

"I said we were here, on the left," he tried to explain.

My dad's right and left confusion had been a source of many family jokes. When I was learning to drive, with my dad in the passenger seat, it was a particular challenge. I learned to respond to incorrect directions with, "Oh, you mean the other left?" My dad saw his left-handedness as a special gift, allowing him coveted corner seats at restaurant tables, his own scissors, and an excuse for his very illegible cursive writing.

"Dad," I felt my eyes begin to sting and my voice trailed off.

"Here she is!" Dad was suddenly waving his arms again.

The Dodge Colt was heading our way. My mother had seen us in the rear-view mirror and turned around. She pulled up next to the Malibu.

Mom nearly flew out of the car, running around the car to the passenger side, while my father slid behind the wheel. I hurled myself into the back seat, like a bank robber in a get-away car.

"I was saying Hail Mary's the whole way," Mom said. "And, you were on the right side," she added, glancing in the backseat to give me a knowing look.

Mom had on her faded black jacket. It was unzipped, thrown over her pink nightgown. The nightie was tucked into her jeans.

For the next 40 minutes or so, Dad drove as if we actually had just robbed a bank.

"Gonna shave a little time off," he said.

The sun winked on the horizon ahead. At last, we whirled into the maze of LaGuardia airline drop-offs. Dad skidded to a stop in a "No Parking" lane and pulled the release to open the empty trunk, just for show, as if we were picking up passenger. Mom and I jumped from the car and ran to the Delta Airlines check-in desk.

"The plane's still here!" I said to Mom amid the noisy hustle of people. "You can go now."

"I'll stay with you until you're on the plane, don't worry. I just want to make sure you get on safely."

Those were the days when non-ticketed visitors could go all the way through the gate. Mom ran with me and gave me a quick hug before boarding. I handed my ticket to the Delta attendant, and nearly skipped down the jetway. How incredible it was that I made it! I settled back into the seat and took a deep breath, exhaling the morning stress in a long sigh.

I had flown commercially twice before in my life. The first time, there was a storm, and the plane circled over, and over, and over, as the pilot waited to be cleared for landing. Up, and down, and around again. Up and down, and around again. I had opened the vomit bag and wished to God I could throw up.

The second time was earlier in the fall. I had an interview at Stony Brook University on Long Island. There was a direct flight from the small Dutchess County airport on Command Airways. It too was harrowing, and I promised myself I would never fly on a prop plane again.

I tried not to think about those nauseating flights as I dug my hand into the seatback in front of me, searching for the barf bag, just in case. The woman in the aisle seat next to me reached into her seatback and handed me her bag.

"Nervous?" She asked.

"No, I'm just not good at flying."

"No one is," she said. "It's unnatural." She put her elbows out like a bird, pretending to fly.

I laughed uneasily. The woman was older than me probably in her 40's, like my parents. She was wearing a blue suit with a colorful scarf. I did not feel like talking and wondered if I should close my eyes. I did not have to pretend to be tired.

"Are you traveling for work?"

"No, I'm going to a medical school interview."

"Like your nephew," she said as she reached across the aisle and poked her finger into the gray padded shoulder of her traveling companion's business suit.

The other woman started to tell us about how her nephew had traveled all over the country for interviews. She was describing how he had one interview on the West Coast and another the next day on the East. She pointed out how he went to every interview. Her story was interrupted by an overhead announcement from the pilot.

"We apologize for the inconvenience. This flight, Flight 840 to National Airport, Washington, DC, has been canceled." The pilot's voice sounded even, but not very apologetic. "We have scheduled another plane, leaving at 10 AM and will do our best to accommodate everyone."

"That's too late!" I turned to the woman next to me, as if she could help.

"Go," she directed me to be the first down the aisle. "Maybe they can get you on something sooner."

I pushed my way to the exit and ran down the jetway, past the spot where, just 15 minutes before, I had hugged Mom. At the desk, I began to explain my dilemma.

"I've got a meeting in DC at 10 o'clock," I explained breathlessly. "Are there any other flights?"

The woman behind the desk looked down, clicking some keys on her computer.

"No, sorry. I can get you on one for tomorrow morning," she offered.

I marveled silently at how she could think tomorrow would be okay, after I had already explained that 10 o'clock today was too late. I leaned forward on the desk and felt my face turn hot.

"Then I need to get my money back," I said.

I did not think GW would offer me a different date and I might just have to give up on an interview with them.

"Sorry. We can give you a voucher for another day, but not your money back."

"I need my money back," I said more loudly. "A voucher won't work for me."

My heart was pounding. My voice was high pitched. I was demanding my money back like an adult, but I sounded like a child.

"I'm sorry," she started to say again, when I heard a voice interrupt her from behind me.

"Give her a refund," a woman said firmly and with authority.

I turned and saw the woman from the seat next to me on the plane. She and her friend had their arms folded defiantly. I looked pleadingly at the woman behind the desk. She did not say a word, and, after a few more clicks, handed me a refund check. I thanked my new friends and they wished me luck as I looked for signs to find the limousine pick-up area. I knew my parents would not be home for another hour, if that, especially after stopping to figure out what to do with the Malibu. My only choice was to call for the limo, with my second quarter.

I used my remaining emergency quarter to contact GW and let them know my flight was canceled and I would not be participating in the interview.

The ride back was thankfully uneventful. I thought about how my parents were likely happily imagining me on my way to DC.

When my parents arrived back to the spot where we left the Malibu, my dad turned the ignition, and it started immediately. Mom later told me that Uncle Charlie, my dad's brother, and his wife, Aunt Diane, decided to drop by for a surprise visit that morning. My parents desperately wanted to go back to sleep when my aunt and uncle showed up at the door, dressed impeccably in new matching safari jackets. Mom, still with her nightgown tucked in her pants, was serving them coffee when I rang the house phone.

I arrived at the designated pick-up spot in Poughkeepsie just before ten o'clock. With no more quarters, I walked straight to the front desk. I leaned toward the attendant.

"I need to use your phone." My voice had an edge of authority, like the woman on the plane.

"Local call?" He asked as he pushed the rotary phone toward me.

"Yes, please." I answered, in my calm, newfound business voice. Mom picked up right away.

"You're there!" Mom's voice rose in excitement as she thought I was calling to say I had arrived in DC and all was well.

"I'm at the Red Roach." Tears welled in my eyes.

The phone was silent as my mom processed this information.

"Dad will be there in a few minutes," she said.

As unlucky has the day had been, I felt very lucky right then.

# 34

## Journey of Beads

### Holly Besaw

In winter of 2016, I was seen at the Emergency Room for a transient cerebral ischemic attack ("minor or mini stroke") and small vessel ischemic disease. It was scary for me with one-sided weakness. I could not move my left hand and had a facial droop on the left side, impacting my speech. The ambulance met us quickly in a parking lot with lights and sirens. The EMT riding with me in the ambulance got IV lines into my arms as we were heading to the hospital. There was one parking spot for ambulances left at the hospital, and they immediately backed into the space.

As soon as we entered, the physician greeted us immediately to assess my ability to move my body parts. My left hand was not able to squeeze or touch the fingers. The Emergency Room team quickly whisked me to the CT area quickly putting me into the machine. A neurologist did a full assessment, checking motor skills as part of the examination. I was embarrassed about not being able to perform all the tasks.

My husband was in the Emergency Room, in a room waiting by himself. He was wondering how I was and where I was. I was back in the CT area, where they told me he was waiting in another room. I was scared because they would not let him be with me. After about

45 minutes, I was taken to meet up with him. We hugged, relieved to see each other. Once we were together, we prayed, "Heavenly Father, Great Physician, thank you for bringing us together again, guiding us to a professional team. We lift our lives up to you for your will. In Jesus' Precious name, Amen."

Blaze, the rescue Italian greyhound, and our two cats greeted us at the door by rubbing on me, sniffing, and tails wagging. I was almost in tears and glad to be back home. At my follow-up visit with the neurologist, a few days later, I had no specific answer for my TIA. We had hoped for an answer.

I developed a headache with left-sided weakness on August 15, 2019. The specialist saw my gait and left arm and suggested we go to a specific Emergency Room and he would call ahead. My husband helped me as we went painstakingly slowly, as I was moving my leg an inch at a time. We contacted my daughter, who was concerned about the situation. She offered to meet us at the hospital, leaving from her county to ours. Traffic was bumper to bumper for both of us to get to the hospital, Don weaving in and out of traffic.

At the Emergency Room, the guard let us park in a close temporary spot; we thanked God, asking for his guidance as we went slowly in. When we went to sign in, the clerk assigned me to a medical team for a complete neurological assessment. I was able to speak, I knew where I was, and I could identify a pen and a watch. They were in such a hurry getting me into the CT machine a nurse almost got run over. CT was ready for me immediately. The CT with contrast showed "mild wall irregularity of the distal cervical right internal carotid artery likely representing evidence of underlying fibromuscular dysplasia (FMD). FMD is a rare condition with abnormal cellular growth in the walls of the medium and large arteries.

My daughter met us at the emergency room to be by our side. The symptoms eventually resolved, praise God. I felt like God was providing us with an answer while having faith on the journey.

On October 14, 2019, I noticed left-sided weakness and conferred with a nurse who suggested I go to the Urgent Care, where I was sent to the hospital by ambulance. Don and I prayed while waiting for the ambulance. The neurologist stated I was outside the 3-hour window for emergency treatment and suggested that I call for an ambulance in the future. The CT with contrast showed "beaded appearance of the right cervical internal carotid artery and very subtle irregularity of the cervical left, compatible with fibromuscular dysplasia."

When compared to August 15, 2019, the heart EKG showed "inferior posterior infraction is now present" (heart attack). We continued to pray, and they kept me overnight. My daughter and husband were there advocating for me while being a support. It was hard not being able to repeat words or touch my nose. The next day, my pets greeted me when I returned home.

I continued as a teacher to make a difference and share the light of the world; it was a challenge, compensating especially with the residual facial droop.

On October 19, I conference called with two providers; I was placed on anti-platelet therapy. I called the Cleveland Clinic advocating for an appointment at an FMD Clinic in November 2019, instead of the usual 1-year wait, a blessing.

November 8, 2019, we arrived at the Cleveland Clinic and were greeted by a valet who parked our car. The facility was enormous, with staff to help us navigate. We met with the doctor, and he listened to the carotid arteries in addition to reviewing previous imaging and confirmed the diagnosis of FMD. I enrolled in the

United States Registry for FMD. I learned I have the multifocal diagnosis, which appears as a "string of beads." I have experienced the common signs and symptoms of FMD, including TIA, stroke, and headaches/migraines, as well as an EKG showing a heart attack.

The clinic staff were amazing with hospitality, including the valet who parked our car, directing us to the office. The doctor was phenomenal. We could see awesome imaging of my heart. We went to the chapel at my alma mater and prayed, thanking God for bringing us to the FMD clinic. The doctor at the clinic personally called us with the results that were not in when we left the FMD clinic. We then had lunch the next day with my sister and mother at my sister's house.

I saw a vascular surgeon when I arrived back in Upstate New York, who referred me to a neurosurgeon. An angiogram was performed by the neurosurgeon on December 31, 2019. The neurosurgeon saw good blood flow and confirmed FMD. I was awake when they did the testing, and I could see the images. I was blessed with no problems during or after the procedure. My husband was with me the entire time. We hugged when we heard I had good blood flow. God is good.

I joined the Fibromuscular Dysplasia Society of America (FMDSA). I had a virtual appointment with the Cleveland Clinic on November 30, 2020. It was recommended against chiropractic manipulation of the cervical spine or roller coasters. I retired December 31, 2020, now volunteering to help disaster victims, along with two pet-assisted therapy cats, visiting in the community, and spending time with grandchildren.

I attended the virtual FMDSA Annual Conference on December 4, 2021. Exercise was mentioned, being careful of lifting weights and yoga/karate moves involving the neck. I make adaptations.

I was able to participate on an FMD Webinar on March 18, 2022. December of 2022, I had an MRI and was sent for CT at the Emergency Room due to an intense headache with left-side weakness. My neurologist came from his office across the street to do an evaluation. One oral medication has been prescribed for some patients to help with the headache symptom. The left-sided weakness began to subside along with the headache after a few hours. We were able to pull the car up to the door of the Emergency Room to get me into the vehicle to go home.

In May 2023, there was an in-person International FMD Conference in Cleveland, Ohio, that I was able to go to with my husband as support. It was a blessing for me to attend with my husband and meet other individuals who have FMD. We got up early and had breakfast at the hotel, then headed downtown in the intense fog.

I wore a butterfly dress and Don a purple polo. We were among the first ones to arrive at the conference, and they had tables set up from FMD Clinics. I was able to visit the tables, then we found seats in the conference room. We were joined by two other individuals with FMD, one from Michigan and the other from Pennsylvania. It was the first time I had the opportunity to meet other individuals with FMD. With FMD, all are happy to learn it is not progressive!

"Headache and Treatment 2023 State of the Art Update" was one of the conference sessions. Some of my migraine headaches have a sensory aura (weakness) and speech and/or language aura. Twenty-seven percent of individuals with FMD have daily headaches, based on information from the United States registry for FMD. I fall into this category. I was able to talk with the presenter personally during a break between sessions, who stated my subset of migraine is not that common, suggesting the same protocol that I currently follow for the headaches that involve sensory and speech/language auras. Each day is different in the intensity of the headaches and whether they have an aura or not. Some days, I have to alter plans. Blessed to have supportive family and knowledgeable medical professionals, I definitely feel a stigma with migraines being an invisible disability. I have one prescription to use for more intense headaches, which requires prior authorization. Today, I pray without ceasing, practice Yoga moves that are safe, take aqua therapy/classes, prayer walks, and volunteer.

For me, life is accepting wherever God places me to care for His people and creatures. I am blessed and fortunate that there were no changes in the imaging in 2021. Procedures are rarely needed, but one has to seek treatment within 30 to 90 minutes if a procedure is needed. I am very careful about avoiding yoga positions, lifting, and do not ride roller coasters; you make adaptations.

This rare condition. FMD has taught me to embrace and enjoy each day, recognizing it is a chance to make a positive difference in God's beautiful world.

# 35

## THE CHIFFOROBE PART 2

### JEAN ANN

By 2011, the four sisters had noticed that their mother had grown frail. They had suggested, perhaps insisted, that she get away from the poison ivy, the unrepaired walkway, the gable vent that the raccoons had breached, the neighbors' bitter lives. They wanted her to move into a continuing care facility.

At first, Marian resisted the idea. After all, her brother Tommy had built the house for her and the girls...after Joe. The house had been their refuge; she couldn't imagine leaving it now. It was her insistent, wistful questions that had kept her there this long. By now, though, her daughters had answers.

"But what about my house?"

She hadn't exactly kept up with it. Solution: Sell it as is.

"But what about Grammy's things in the basement? You girls might want some of it." Marian liked the idea of the girls wanting her mother's table.

Solution: Let us take what we want; call someone to take the rest.

"But it costs money to live in the new place."

Solution: There's enough.

Once she allowed her unresolved questions to be answered, Marian was free, whether she wanted to be or not.

To support their mother, the middle daughters, Dar and Audie, set upon the main floor of the house to excavate what lay beneath the familiar surface. Emmy braved the attic, Jeannie the basement. Space by space, they separated what was to go to Marian's new home from what was to be hauled to the end of the driveway on garbage day. At last, some boxes full of things that Marian wanted, sat resolutely next to a few pieces of empty furniture—Marian's since childhood.

Finally, only the garage was left to exhume. One day, Audie's son, Marty, who was 21, and Jeannie decided to take it on. Neither nephew nor aunt would have attempted it without the other. When they opened the garage door and saw what was inside, Marty's face said it all. His parents had kept a reasonably orderly garage.

Jeannie sighed, looking around at the debris, then at Marty, and offered, "Well, this is what she could manage."

"Yeah, I know."

Jeannie and Marty bagged much of the contents of the garage by the end of the day. There were blistered cardboard bumper signs for the summer attractions in upstate New York—Gaslight Village, Storytown. Back when the girls were little, parking lot attendants would use wire to attach the bumper signs to the ocean of visiting cars. There was the cracked rear-view mirror that attached to the driver's side door. Marian had once relied on it to see behind their pop-up trailer on the highway—during the summers that they went camping...after Joe. There were frames of lawn chairs whose webbed seats had long since worn away. Screws with no threads, bent nails. Smashed lamps. Severed extension cords. Torn, faded posters of pop stars, of ballerinas, of verdant country scenery.

Some things didn't fit in bags. A menagerie of ghostly hardware: a pitchfork and rake with split, rotted handles. An ancient, crippled sewing machine. Rusty bike skeletons. All of it had been marinating in decades of moisture with added measures of dirt and dust. Jeannie and Marty left bags of junk neatly lined up inside the garage door; beside it, they put the rest. Whoever could help haul it all to the road on garbage day would have no confusion: it was all going.

In the worst corner of the garage was the filthy old pink chifforobe. The wretched thing was covered in sticky spider webs that clung around every surface, as if to affix one neglected plane of it to the next. Marty had barely seen the chifforobe before; he had no attachment to it, no opinion about it. Jeannie noted that it was in two pieces. One piece amounted to most of the chifforobe—except for a gaping hole where one of the drawers used to be. Not even a maimed drawer had turned up anywhere.

The other piece was its own closet door, torn off and leaning up against it. Across the door was a child's scrawl in thick, red crayon. Jeannie didn't remember that. She reckoned that she couldn't have written on the chifforobe door. Way back then, she would have known she shouldn't. Maybe Emmy...?

In her reverie, an indistinct memory floated back—the day they'd hidden Emmy in the chifforobe.

"Mommy, we looked all over, and we can't find Emmy," the older girls had told Marian, who played along.

"Can't find Emmy? That can't be! Where could she be?"

Marian went in search of her littlest daughter. Her zoris clapped the soles of her feet as she kept up her soliloquy about where Emmy might be. When she neared the chifforobe, poor missing Emmy popped the closet door open.

"I'm here, Mommy!" she said sweetly.

"There you are! We thought you were lost!" Marian sighed.

She hugged Emmy tenderly, as the older sisters gratefully acknowledged her return.

The girls had been working on Marian's house for weeks. Convinced that Marian could have saved things that would have been of interest, Jeannie had insisted on going through everything carefully. The sisters had been meticulous, perhaps to a fault, and Jeannie had indeed found gems. Now even she was ready to be done with the house. The last of it was the garage; the last of that, the chifforobe. The dirty, broken thing had been in the family for nearly 80 years. All four sisters had used it when they were babies. But as they had grown older, they'd all had different furniture, discarded years before. So, it seemed logical to ditch the chifforobe. But Jeannie couldn't bring herself to ask Marty to help her move it close to the rest of the stuff destined for the end of the driveway. Instead, Jeannie asked him to vacuum all its surfaces. She would follow with Formula 409. By the time they were done, Jeannie figured she'd be able to let the chifforobe go. She just...had to work through it.

But the plan didn't work. Try as she might to embrace the sensible view, Jeannie felt the opposite pull: to take the chifforobe back, to reclaim it, to help her set things right, and erase the grief, the pain of the father having left them all on their own—the mother and the four little girls—when they had no defenses.

Instead of putting the chifforobe with the rest of the junk, Jeannie and Marty put it in Jeannie's car. When she left Long Island, she thought that at some point during the six hours it took to get back to central New York, she might convince herself to get rid of it. If not, she trusted that she would eventually be presented with a price she wouldn't pay to preserve the thing.

It might be when she had to take it out of the car; it was too bulky, too heavy. It might be when she had to prepare a space for it in her own garage; there wasn't much room. It might be when she would watch her husband watch her quizzically, wondering what she was up to as she labored over the thing. There would be something—some line—and she'd recognize it, and when she got to that line, she'd make the chifforobe disappear.

Once she pulled into her driveway, Jeannie had to admit that she was a little embarrassed to have driven the chifforobe six hours from one garage so it could sit in another garage. Not enough to regret having done it, though.

A few weeks later, in late spring, despite all the things that could have rightly distracted her from the chifforobe, she found herself on the phone with someone who could repair and refinish it. Jim came highly recommended. He would come to see it on Friday, he said, and he wouldn't charge for the visit. It was only if she hired him, and he brought the finished piece back that she'd pay anything. Filled as she was with ambivalence—the chifforobe was a certified piece of junk and could never be anything else—or could it?—it was lucky for her that Jim had a disarming demeanor, kind eyes, and decades of experience in the furniture industry.

In the garage, Jeannie was nervous. She gestured tentatively toward the chifforobe.

"Do you think this...could this thing...be nice?" she asked Jim hesitantly, safe enough to ask, but bracing, in case he shook his head at the sight of the chifforobe and chuckled.

But Jim looked at the chifforobe the way a gardener looks at a disappointing plant, and even a little like he was defending it.

"Well, it's not gorgeous, but part of it is that milk paint on it. Now if it was stained, it would be a huge improvement. Even if it was painted with modern paint, it would be better. See, when this piece was new, milk paint was the available paint and it's a pain in the neck to get it off these pieces. That's what costs the money."

What about the drawer?

"I could make one to match the others exactly. That's no problem."

The door...?

"That's nothing. I can fix it and put it back on."

By the time Jim left, Jeannie realized that he was a sort of counselor. He listened attentively, waiting to get a sense of what Jeannie wanted. He answered her questions, but only when asked did he add his informed perspective. He didn't give direct advice or push either way. He estimated that it would cost about 1,500 dollars to bring the chifforobe back—to make it perfect. The estimate was good for a year.

It would have been easier if Jim had proclaimed the project a fool's errand; what he said left everything on the table. Jeannie visualized 15 stacks of dollar bills, 100 per stack. It was a small fortune, but she could pay it. The more she thought she shouldn't, the more she couldn't forget the chifforobe's story. It had been in her grandmother's home from when her Aunt Glo was born. Years later, her own parents had driven it to their Virginia home and used it for Jeannie and her sisters. Within two days of their father Joe's death, the girls and their mother had been moved to Long Island. A day later, the chifforobe, like their clothes, the breakfront, and the pictures on the walls had been packed up and shipped there, too.

Seeing the red crayon brought back its familiarity and the vulnerability of each of the baby girls that the chifforobe had been used for.

With the impending decision in her lap, Jeannie consulted her mother, her sisters, her friends and her Aunt Glo to ask what they would do. It was unanimous: it was too expensive for a such a pathetic piece. Jeannie wanted to agree, wanted to believe that the chifforobe meant nothing. But it was getting to her. As it sat in Jeannie's garage awaiting a verdict, it seemed to be cajoling her in an inarticulate, disfigured way.

"Keep me," it seemed to whisper weakly, "and I'll help you."

Jeannie heard it, even as she shook it off. The wounded chifforobe sat and sat. The more Jeannie looked at it, the more she saw how sad and broken it was. But there was something that Jim had said the day he'd come.

"If you want to preserve it, you can have it like new. People do that because things have sentimental value. I bet it would be beautiful once that paint is off. It's worth what you think it's worth. Take some time to think about it. Don't rush."

His words wafted into her brain as the chifforobe drifted into her heart. When the daffodils came up, Jeannie found herself on the phone again. A few days later, Jim came to get the chifforobe. She told him to take all the time he needed. He was so busy in his shop that there was no word from him for months.

That was fine with Jeannie. She had her doubts, anyway. Even though it was worth a try, in the end, if Jim didn't bring her back a chifforobe, so be it. Anything could happen. She imagined that he might leave his shop one day to go home, only to return the next day to find that it had flooded in the spring rains or burned down in the summer heat. She imagined he might call her apologetically one day to tell her that the chifforobe was gone.

If that happened, Jeannie would be magnanimous. She'd tell him that the loss of the chifforobe was of no consequence at all. It was enough that they'd both tried to bring it back. After all, the chifforobe was just a symbol; fixing it fixed nothing. Jeannie and her sisters still went through their childhoods in anguish because their father had died. They'd had no choice but to steep in the realization that when someone dies, no matter how you beg them to come home, they don't. Without their father, their mother was the most alone person that they had ever known.

The next year, after the daffodils wilted, Jim called. But he didn't say that the chifforobe had been lost in an innocent little natural disaster. He didn't say that he had begun the job and realized that it would cost way more. Like 10,000 dollars. Surely if he said that, Jeannie would have known the answer: hack the chifforobe apart and use it for firewood, or grist for something more important, grander than her trifling childhood, and the problems that her father's departure had set in motion.

But none of that happened. Jim called to say that the chifforobe was ready, it was gorgeous, and that he could bring it on Friday.

# 36

## GROWING UP IN WEICHANG

### APPLE AN

Across the street from the bus station, a gigantic billboard stood between two 3-story buildings, and a half-body portrait of Chairman Mao smiled at us. The portrait was the tallest I have ever seen of Chairman Mao, and I have seen many of them in the eight years of my life.

I craned my neck way back, mesmerized. Chairman Mao—depicted realistically compared to many other portraits—was waving his right hand and wearing a grass-green uniform with a red banner on his left arm. His hat carried a bright red star on the front.

"Your brother painted that portrait," Aunt Qi said to Mom.

Middle-aged, a few centimeters shorter and a few years younger than Mom, Qi had darker skin and two long, thick, braided pigtails that reached her bottom. She brought two boys and a girl to greet us at the bus station.

*What?! Wow! My uncle did this! Wow! He must be so talented and so trusted by the Communist Party! He must be a famous person.*

My admiration of an uncle I had never seen soared.

"This is where it happened?" asked Mom.

"Yeah. He was doing a final touch. If you look carefully, you can see the brush mark on that corner." Qi pointed to the portrait.

"Yes, I see. Can no one finish it?" asked Mom.

"None in this region has that skill, and none dared to do it after what happened to him a year ago," Qi replied.

I listened and examined the portrait. I did not see any imperfection marks.

"It must be tough on you to take care of him and your three children. Thank you for taking my two girls."

In the fall of 1971, Mom had to co-lead a project to build a dam in a remote place with no schools, stores, houses, or roads. Her team was to live in tents for a year. Dad attended a camp for reeducation. Mom's brother Xi-Dan and his wife Qi agreed to let my 7-year-old sister and me live with them in Weichang, a small town in Heibei Province.

"It's tough. But we manage. Plus, children help with house chores."

"Aren't they too young?" asked Mom.

"Yin is four months older than Apple, eight now. The girl, Xiaozhi, is six, and Wawa five."

Qi turned to look at me and Shanshan. "Do you want to learn to help?"

A feeling of being a mature person and of importance occurred to me. Shanshan must feel the same way. We both said, "Yes!"


"That is where we live." Qi pointed to the hill at the end of the road.

Two stories higher than the street level, the yard sat at the top of the stairs. The 15 steps ran along the hill on one side and were wide open on the other side with no fence or rail guard.

*Will someone fall off the steps?* I wondered while climbing up, carrying the bags with effort.

A man stood at the top of the stairs. A grin covered his face. That must be Uncle.

"Baba, Baba!" Wawa ran up with no trouble and embraced Xi-Dan's legs. Xi-Dan patted the top of Wawa's head, then moved aside to let the rest of us enter the yard. He didn't offer anyone a hand to take the bags from them.

Xi-Dan was much taller than most men and had a straight back and wide shoulders. He had a military-style short haircut. A skillful hairdresser with clippers could do it within 10 minutes. I learned later that Qi cut his and the children's hair, just as Mom cut our hair.

Xi-Dan's eyes twinkled behind the lenses. He spoke little and had an authoritative air. I got the sense that he came from another world, had read many books, and had many brilliant ideas. *How lucky is Aunt?* I glanced at Qi, who looked plain and insignificant.

Upon further examination, I saw Uncle wearing a special vest around his upper body on this hot day. The metal vest held his upper body straight and prevented him from bending or twisting. He took off the vest only for sleep. He could not walk very far and rarely left his house. His injury prevented him from working, so he took only half of his salary home.

After entering the house, Qi put on her apron. Yin set up the fire on the stove in the outside room. Xiaozi pulled and pushed the handle of the box fan to keep the fire going. Yin put water in a big pot and covered it with a steamer. Qi mixed cornmeal and wheat flour into dough and made round buns to put in the steamer. Once the steamer was done, Qi added spices and dried vegetables into the boiling water to make it a soup. Then she stir-fried a mix of fresh and pickled vegetables into a dish.

In the yard, Wawa gathered stools to surround a small square table on the ground.

"Baba, how many stools?"

"Can you count how many people?" Xi-Dan asked.

Wawa put the six stools he found. "Baba, we need two more."

Xi-Dan smiled. "Correct. Use these two stumps from the tree we cut last year. Tomorrow after your Aunt leaves, we just need one of them."

"Yes, that will make seven of us!"

Wawa set up the bowls and chopsticks.

Everyone sat. The only sounds were chewing and swallowing the soup. When Mom, Shanshan, and I still had half of the buns in our hands and soup in our bowls, the five members of the Uncle's family already finished their meal.

That became a pattern. During waking hours, mealtime was the only time no one talked. There was only one dish on the small table, surrounded by seven of us. Shanshan and I learned that if we were shy or slow, we would have half-empty stomachs.

We both became fast eaters.

At night, everyone slept on the same warm kang that occupied half of the inner room and was heated by the cooking stove. Xi-Dan took the very end of the kang, next to a wide window stand that held a large fish tank containing 10 tropical fish. Qi slept on the other end along the wall that divided the two rooms.

"I want to sleep next to Xiaozi!" Shanshan exclaimed.

"Sure. You girls sleep next to me. Wawa sleeps next to his dad." Qi directed.

"Where do you sleep?" I asked Yin.

His face turned red, and he pointed to the bottom next to the two windows.

"He sleeps there sideways because he wets the bed," said Qi.

Within the first week of arrival, Qi took the three girls to the public bathhouse.

People overran the bathhouse. It had a vast pool filled with burning hot water. With water that hot, the pool was inaccessible, a condition that may have been deliberate to keep the water clean. Qi brought a basin to mix hot water with cool water to use. To my delight, Qi didn't bother using the few showerheads.

Upon coming back from the public bathhouse, Qi said to me, "You'll wash the dirty clothes."

I had never done that. Mom did the laundry at home. Qi did not instruct me on how to do it, and I didn't ask, because I had watched Mom do it. I gathered the dirty clothes, emptied the pockets, and put them in a metal bowl. After adding water, I scrubbed each item on a wooden washboard, wrung it out, and hung it on the line. I was proud watching the clothesline full. I washed seven people's dirty clothes!

Qi came to the yard and checked two pieces. "Did you use soap?"

Oops, I didn't. I was so embarrassed. I gathered the clothes back into the bowl and redid everything by applying soap and rubbing hard. My hands became red and itchy by the time I finished.

Washing clothes for the whole family became my responsibility. It was brutal in the winter because I had to use icy water.

My other solo responsibility was washing the hair of the three girls. Despite admiring Qi's long braided hair that reached her rear end, I found short hair much more practical to wash.

The countryside surrounding the small town offered a unique experience. One day, all five kids journeyed to gather tree branches and bushes on the hills and valleys behind the house. They made good firewood for cooking. Shanshan and Xiaozi stayed together, goofing around and laughing out loud. Yin took Wawa to find branches to make a sword or a gun.

I wandered around by myself, admiring the wild plants and flowers on the curvy landscape. Then I saw small dirt piles the height of my waist next to each other. There were brown-colored papers pressed on top of them by rocks.

Paper! What a waste to put it here. It'd be great for writing or the bathroom. I took the sheets home and proudly showed them to everyone at home.

"Those dirt piles are graves. People put these papers to show they miss the dead ones. You should put them back," said Qi.

The hair stood up on the back of my neck. The next day, I put the papers back. "Please don't be angry with me," I pled to those under the dirt and those who put the papers up.

For a long time, brown paper reminded me of the instance.

Getting water was one of the most challenging chores, especially on winter days, which were plentiful since Weichang was in the north of China. The closest well was a 15-minute walk away.

Qi stood on the narrow edge surrounding the opening of the reel well. She threw the wooden bucket connected to the roller into the deep hole. The first time I stood on the edge, I fainted at the sight of the darkness inside the well.

As the rope straightened, Qi turned the handle to roll the rope onto the roller, and the bucket came to the surface. Qi pulled it over to the edge and then poured water into our buckets to be carried home. During the winter, ice from the splashed water covered the edge, making standing there dangerous.

Qi used a pole on her shoulder to carry two buckets. The two ends of the pole had metal chains to secure the buckets. She had to switch shoulders and take breaks from time to time during the walk home.

Yin and I were too short and weak to carry a bucket. We used a flat stick to carry one big bucket on our shoulders. Yin was in the front, and I followed because he was shorter than me. We synchronized our steps so that the water wouldn't spill while walking home.

Climbing the 15 steps was challenging. Yin lowered the stick to his hands to prevent the water bucket from sliding toward my end.

Once we got into the outer room, Qi lifted the lighter bucket and dumped the water into an enormous water tank, which was the height of my waist. It could hold the water from two trips. If Qi was too tired, she directed me to use a big water scoop to move water from the bucket to the tank.

During our entire stay, Uncle did little housework, and didn't even express his appreciation and gratitude. My opinion of him took a turn when he changed his fish tank once a week, with the water we put so much effort into bringing home. The significance of his being talented and handsome faded in my mind. I grew fond of Qi, who carried the entire family on her shoulders.

Eleven months after arriving at Weichang, Mom took us back. A Chinese proverb states, "Children from poor families grow up fast." My year in Weichang proved that.

## 37

# Cats, Birds and Souls

### Reverend Andrea Abbott

This past summer, our house was the site of an invasion. My husband and I enjoy watching the birds. We have squirrel-proof feeders, hummingbird feeders, thistle feeders, tube feeders and two fountains that keep fresh water running for the birds' bathing pleasure. We planted flowers that are attractive to birds and are well known at our local feed store where we purchase large bags of sunflower seeds. We've attracted the usual crowd: chickadees, cardinals, blue jays, finches of all sorts, orioles, woodpeckers, titmice, sparrows, grackles (lots of grackles), and doves. By the way, contrary to their reputations as birds of peace, doves take over the feeders and push out the little birds. We don't get really exotic birds but we enjoy watching our guests while they dine, even if we're not going to be calling the Audubon Society with a rare find. However, for at least the past year, our enjoyment has been drastically curtailed. Our neighbor's cats have seen us as a bistro, a gourmet paradise, or at least as a reliable diner.

The neighbors in question live one house away from us and have lived there longer than we have. We don't know them well, just enough to wave to and exchange greetings. We know that they are a middle-aged couple and are rumored to have at least seven cats. We don't see the entire cattery in our garden, but two of the cats, a marmalade and a long-haired black cat, are there almost every day. In the past, though they have always had cats, we have not had any difficulties with them. Either previous cats were sneakier or just weren't interested in freshly prepared chickadee. But these two cats are real hunters. If we could have, somehow, prevailed on them to concentrate on mice, which we often have in plenty, we might have reached some sort of détente. But these two like catching birds.

We have never had neighbor problems and really did not want to start some kind of unpleasantness. We know how people can feel about any criticism of their pets. When we had beloved dogs, we, too, felt they could do no wrong. We also know our neighbors are responsible people who love their cats. We know that the cats are well cared for and well-fed. Unfortunately, if you are a cat, or perhaps if you are a cat of a particular temperament, it doesn't matter if you are well-fed. The urge to hunt is almost irresistible. It is a huge part of being a cat, a form of expression like a human's need for purpose. So how could birds, cats, and humans all just get along?

Unwittingly, we had an intermediary in our first set of negotiations. We had mentioned some of our troubles to one of the people in the house between us and the house where the cats reside. We hadn't asked these neighbors to intervene as diplomats, but they did and we were told the cat owners tried to moderate their cats' behavior. Since we are talking about innate instincts, it was not terribly successful.

We kept watch, running out into the garden and yelling like demented things whenever we saw a cat. This meant that a lot of our time was taken up at windows or staking out the patio. Just like those obsessed with invasions of all kinds, our time was spent less and less enjoying our garden and more and more on guard.

Then two incidents occurred that ratcheted up the war. The first was that we watched helplessly as the black cat caught and devoured a chickadee before we could rush to its rescue. The second was that twice we found our fancy fountain/birdbath tipped over, possibly by cats jumping to get a bird. It was chipped and parts were broken. My husband was able to fix it but it will never look the same.

We still didn't want to confront our neighbors. We have lived in our house and enjoyed our neighborhood for many years. Also, we were baffled about a solution. Should we ask our neighbors to keep their cats in? Wouldn't they insist that cats, perhaps particularly these cats, have no meaningful existence if they have to stay indoors? Did we have an answer for this that didn't involve what might be seen as incarceration, loss of catly liberty, an abrogation of catly rights? We were at a loss for the humane and yet effective solution. I went around humming, "Cats gotta pounce and birds gotta die." Sad and torn.

Because, the fact is, we both like cats. I'm allergic to them, and to birds, too, by the way, but I've enjoyed warm, if physically distant, relationships with many cats over the years. But the fact remains that all cats, feral cats particularly, account for a huge number of wild bird deaths. The wild bird population is decreasing while the cat population seems to be doing very well. However, peace with neighbors was a priority for us.

So, instead of confrontation, we built a wall. Yes, a wall. In our defense, we didn't think our neighbors would pay for it. We also were somewhat limited in our ability to build something truly effective. Have you any idea what kind of expense would be involved in walling out cats? So we settled for a deterrent. We bought netting and loosely attached it to boards to shut off the alley where the cats lurked until they were ready to pounce. We hoped that this would make our garden less attractive.

Then we found ourselves worrying about the cats getting caught up in the netting. So we had to stay close to home to keep checking that they weren't helplessly bound up. We needn't have worried. The first cat to get through pulled down the netting in quick order and escaped unscathed.

Then, all our good intentions of peace with our neighbors went up in smoke. We saw our neighbor as she was getting groceries out of her car and we told her about the chickadee incident and the fountain incident and she responded, rather flippantly, "I'll give you a squirt gun." We were seething! What an inadequate response! How uncaring! And, besides that, did the only solution have to involve arming ourselves?

For what seemed like a long time after this, we went out of our way to avoid them. I think they were also avoiding us and it was very awkward. I wondered what, if anything, the resolution might be. Would it escalate? How could it be resolved? My initial feelings of anger gave way to feelings of sadness. It wasn't like losing a friend, but it was painful.

Then, something gave me a chance to resolve the situation. Our street was paved and everyone had to park on the cross street. One day, as I was getting out of my car, I noticed that my neighbor parked right behind me and got out of her car at just the same time. We both looked the other way to avoid eye contact and then I thought, "This is silly." I said something to her about having to walk farther with groceries and hoping the paving would be done soon. She looked relieved and agreed and then said, "How much did your fountain cost? I think we should replace it."

I told her that we didn't want her to replace it. She said she was sorry the cats had done this. I said we had also been worried about the cats being crushed by the fountain as it fell. We agreed it was a problem, cats being cats and birds being birds. We came to no solution, but I left feeling better just because she had been concerned and I think she felt better too. We aren't any closer to each other but we wave at each other and greet each other again and that is good enough for me. Mostly, I'm glad that I'm not feeling angry anymore.

Often, I find, there is no definitive solution. Only in the movies, perhaps, are there decisive victories, the triumph of the heroes over the villains. Much more often we are left with incomplete solutions to situations that are more complicated than we imagined. Even when we seem to win, we find that the victory is not as sweet as we had imagined. We find we do not really want to reduce our opponent to ashes. We find that we are faced with the problem of what to do with the defeated. We find that mercy and kindness are far greater virtues than we thought they were in our moments of wrath.

In Dante's great poem, the Divine Comedy, he pictures the realm of purgatory, where souls expiate the sins they committed on earth. There are nine stages in purgatory, and the third terrace is for people who were wrathful in life. They wander forever blinded by black smoke, an analogy for the anger that blinded them in life. When I was less angry, I realized that cats are only a problem to birds because humans, have upset the balance of nature. As our homes invade woodlands, we, and our cats, encroach on the songbirds' homes. Also, irresponsible humans do not spay or neuter their cats and, all too often, they abandon their cats when they are tired of them, leaving them to become feral. I also remembered that the destruction of the world's rainforests has done more to deplete the bird population than anything else. Cats are only being cats when they pounce on chickadees. As far as we know, we are unique in the animal kingdom for our great ability to transcend instinct, to be able to choose much of how we live, and even more, how we think and react to things.

We are nearly at an end to this shaggy cat story and the real question it asks is how can we all get along, cats, birds, and souls? We have competing needs and desires. We live in a political climate that encourages us to be angry with those who compete for resources, for those who seem to threaten our needs and desires. We also know that anger against others is more satisfying than anger at ourselves and is much more satisfying than sadness. Anger and sadness weave in a devil's dance and it takes a lot to get us off that dance floor. In addition, as I found, anger creates its own sadness of ruptured relationships. So how do we end this invitation to mutual madness?

Mutual coexistence doesn't have the ring of more noble words like truth or triumph or justice but after a week or so of feeling at odds with my neighbor, it will do for me. The thick smoke of my anger is gone and, without it, I find the summer sun shining and the world again a sparkling place. Perhaps in this place, we can find a way that cats, birds, and humans can find balance. In this shared quest, I find peace.

# About the Editors

**Apple An** is an award-winning author, professor, and historian whose stories explore migration, cultural memory, and the quiet strength of women through times of upheaval. She writes under her pen name to celebrate her Chinese heritage and share universal truths. Apple lives in Baldwinsville, New York, where she balances storytelling, scholarship, and a lifelong love of movement and learning. Find more about Apple An and her creative work at www.AppleAnBooks.com.

**Georgia A. Popoff** is a writer, editor, arts-in-education specialist, and program coordinator for the YMCA of Central NY's Writers Voice, where she teaches poetry and creative nonfiction. Her fourth collection of poetry, *Psychometry*, released in late 2019 by Tiger Bark Press, was a finalist for Utica College's Eugene Nassar Poetry Prize and the CNY Book Award for Poetry. Tiger Bark Press released her fifth collection, *Living with Haints* in spring 2024. In 2022, Georgia was named Poet Laureate of Onondaga County for a 2-year term of service. She is the series editor for the University of Michigan Press *Under Discussion* book series on contemporary poets. Visit www.georgiapopoff.com and follow her on Facebook, Instagram, and Twitter: @gappoet.

# About the Contributors

**April Williamson** currently resides in Syracuse, NY, where she moved in 2008 after growing up in the deep south. She has been a science teacher in the city for the past 10 years. April joined the Downtown Writer's Center in 2022 and has been sharing stories from her life since.

**Ren vanMeenen** teaches at Rochester Institute of Technology. She is the Editor of *Afterimage* and has published in several other publications. She holds Master's degrees in Transformative Language Arts and Media Studies; is competing a PhD in Philosophy, Art and Critical Thought; and is a certified writing therapist.

**Sophia Tejeiro** grew up on Long Island and now makes her home in Central New York, where she balances motherhood, librarianship, and a lifelong love of the mystical. A former yoga teacher and aspiring writer, she seeks to weave wonder into the fabric of everyday life.

**Francesca Swick** is a writer in perpetual pursuit of whimsy. She is currently working on a book of personal essays, though she once drafted a romantic comedy screenplay out of pure spite. She is the Paralibrarian for Art & Digital Communications at the DeWitt & Jamesville Library. You can find her online at francesca.swick on Instagram.

**Jackie Southard**, from upstate New York, lives in Greer, SC, with her husband of 40 years, Mike. Their sons, Ryan and Scott, and Scott's wife, Laura, live nearby, keeping family close. This piece is from Jackie's memoir, a collection of humorous stories written for her precocious, imaginative, and creative sons.

**Dyana Smolen** is a professional writer with decades of experience. Trained as a journalist, she's published hundreds of news articles and contributed to several online magazines. Currently, she applies her storytelling skills to support nonprofits, finding joy in making a positive difference. Dyana enjoys nonfiction essay writing and aspires to one day assemble her work into a book. She lives in Oneida, NY.

**Lisa Sellin** is retired from corporate and government HR work. She has lived abroad in Thailand, Madagascar, Vietnam, Oman, Afghanistan, and Germany, but is happily re-establishing an affection for Central New York. She has taken writing classes throughout her adult life and is now focusing her writing on autobiographical pieces.

**Jacqueline Schmitt.** Generations of my family have lived in Central New York. This essay is part of an extended conversation with the past and what it means to inherit part of this beautiful but contested ground. I give belated thanks to the Onondaga Nation for their stewardship of our shared legacy.

**Lee B. Savidge**, award-winning author and poet, retired engineer, military veteran, Rensselaer Polytechnic Institute and Syracuse University graduate, active in Syracuse, New York, writing groups. He is published in anthologies, *The Weight Of My Armor* (Parlor Press, 2017), *What We See On Our Journeys* and *Earth Care* (Willet Press, 2021, 2022), and *28 Voices* (Voices Heard Publishing, 2024).

**Kathy Rothenberg** is a retired schoolteacher who lives in Liverpool, NY. She is currently writing a memoir that includes her experiences growing up in the Eastwood area of Syracuse. Her nonfiction short story, *Halfway There,* appeared in the 2022 edition of *Stone Canoe.*

**Georgia A. Popoff** teaches for the YMCA of Central NY's Writers Voice and serves as Poet Laureate of Onondaga County, NY (2022-2025). Her fifth collection is Living with Haints (Tiger Bark Press, 2024). She is the editor for the University of Michigan Press Under Discussion book series on contemporary poets.

**Aaron M. Perrine** is a lifelong upstate New Yorker who has settled in the Eastwood neighborhood of Syracuse with his wife and son. This is his second published piece. He works on his own writing when he isn't trying to ensure the writing of others is correct.

**Mary J. Nowyj** is an Onondaga Hill resident. She taught Communication Skills at OCC. During her time as the Town Of Onondaga historian, she wrote articles and published an Arcadia Image book of various hamlets. She enjoys theater, traveling, and volunteering for non-profit organizations.

**Sam Netzband** is a romance author of four novels, which are in the process of being published. She is crafting her first nonfiction book that details her journey to all fifty states. She is a member of Romance Writers of America and a graduate of the Romance Author Mentorship Program.

**Marissa Montgomery** is an academic writer who lives in Central New York. This contribution is the sequel to her piece in *28 Voices.* Her years researching the historical and cultural roots of systemic misogyny led her to write about her own life experiences. This piece is part of larger memoir that demonstrates the power of dreamwork to free women from repetitive cycles of abuse.

**Nilsa Evie Mariano** graduated Binghamton University with a Masters in Comparative Literature. At heart, she is a Brooklyn girl. Nilsa was published in *Muleskinner, Five Minute, Wildgreens,* and *Stone Canoe.* She is proud of being published in the inaugural edition of *Chicken Soup for the Latino Soul.* Nilsa likes crushed ice.

**Linda Loomis**. Writer-teacher Loomis contributes a coming-of-age story about her son, a medical doctor, and his twin sisters. She directed the journalism program and taught creative writing at SUNY Oswego, has been a reporter/editor for community and college publications, is a contributing writer for Syracuse.com/The Post-Standard, and volunteers as a writing workshop presenter.

**Karen Foresti Hempson** is a retired professor of Social Studies Education. Her two books, *Bean Pickers: American Immigrant Portraits*, and *Shellback*, are based on true stories. Writing competitions recognized her work with numerous awards and recognitions. Several of her essays were published in anthologies and professional journals.

**Felicia Haury** is a writer and lifelong learner who hails from San Diego, California. In 2024, she was featured in *28 Voices*. She is currently working on a memoir about her beloved sister. feliciahaury@yahoo.com

**Indu Gupta** is a physician and former Onondaga County Health Commissioner. She has witnessed firsthand the pain, suffering and triumphs of everyday people. Besides her parents and family, she credits these intimate experiences in making her a caring human being. She always wanted to bring those stories to life. The writing workshop opened that door.

**Samuel D. Gruber** is an architectural historian, historic preservationist, and community activist. He has written books, chapters, reports, articles, and blogs about Jewish, medieval, and modern art and architecture, and lectures widely. Sam has lived in Syracuse's Westcott neighborhood, about which he is writing a book, since 1994.

**Mary C. Gillen**, Mexico, NY, is a participant in the YMCA of CNY's Writers Voice PRO Program. Published in anthologies including *28 Voices* and *Stone Canoe*, she is working on a YA chapbook and a short story. Mary is a member of Sisters in Crime, Queer Crime Writers, and Short Mystery Fiction Society.

**Vincenza Freeborn,** born in 1958, is one of eleven children raised by a single mother. She holds a BS in Psychology from SUNY New Paltz and an MSW from Adelphi University, and operates a private psychotherapy practice in Albany, NY. She enjoys cultivating her creative writing and loves bass fishing!

**Kathy Ferro** is a retiree who worked as an administrative assistant for several non-profits in the Syracuse area. She is taking her first foray into writing, hoping to capture the brief but incredibly powerful journey of accompanying her parents as they grappled with physical and mental decline in their final years.

**D'Arcy Farlow** is a facilitator and strategic planner who has spent most of her career promoting healthy communities and organizations. She has supported a broad range of groups to envision a better future and to work collaboratively to achieve that future. D'Arcy is writing a memoir about the adventures of living in London, England, during the early years of her marriage.

**Nancy Avery Dafoe**, poet/author/educator, has 15 published books, with the most recent including poetry collection *When Mine Canaries Stop Singing* (FLP, June 2024), novels *Yet in the Land of the Living* (Wings ePress, 2024) and *Socrates is Dead Again* (PWP, 2021), and a memoir *Unstuck in Time* (PWP, 2021).

**Andrea Cifonelli** is a member of The Writer's Voice of CNY. She is the recipient of Upstate Medical University's 2025 Dearing Writing Award and is published in their literary journal, *The Healing Muse.* Andrea believes in the power of storytelling and writes in honor of her late brother, Danny. Andrea's children, Simon and Oscar, are her inspiration.

**Tracy Chamberlain Higginbotham** is an entrepreneur, feminist, activist, and writer. She is a two-time Small Business Administration Women in Business Champion of the Year. Her book, *Under a Rose-Colored Hat,* highlights living with alopecia and kindness demonstrated by strangers. She is married with two sons and one granddaughter – Ivy Rose.

**Hayley Marama Cavino**, Ph.D, was born in Aotearoa/New Zealand. She has taught at Ithaca College, Colgate University, Syracuse University, and the University of Waikato. She is of Māori, Irish, Jewish, Scottish, and English descent and currently splits her time between her ancestral lands in Tauranga Moana and Haudenosaunee Territory.

**Daniel Callahan** has enjoyed creative writing since elementary school. The thing he loves most about creative nonfiction is that he does not have to come up with story ideas since he has already lived them! As a high school English teacher, he loves spreading his joy of reading and writing.

**Deborah Young Bradshaw** is a physician and writer who grew up in Central New York. She was raised on a dairy farm and writes about her family. Her work has appeared in *Stone Canoe, The Healing Muse, The Annals of Internal Medicine,* and *Neurology.* Her memoir piece, *Dry Cows,* was named a 2020 finalist in the *Jeffrey E. Smith Editor Prize for the Missouri Review.*

**April Bradley** has previously been published in *The Healing Muse*. She works in health care and lives in Syracuse, NY, with her husband, children, and Great Dane.

**Ann Botash** is a pediatrician, writer, and SUNY Distinguished Teaching Professor at SUNY Upstate Golisano Children's Hospital in Syracuse, NY. A Vassar graduate and Poughkeepsie native, she specializes in child abuse care and has received national recognition for teaching and child advocacy. She finds joy in writing and time with family.

**Holly Besaw** is a lay servant, pet-therapy volunteer, and retired educator who lives in rural Upstate New York. She is author of a rare-disease poem and two books for the children she visits with her therapy cats. Deeply religious, Besaw draws her strength and inspiration from her faith.

**Jean Ann** is a retired linguist who is finding the words to tell the stories of her family of origin. She is thrilled to contribute The Chifforobe Part 2 to this volume; it continues the story of The Chifforobe Part 1, which appeared in *28 Voices*.

**Apple An** grew up in China and came to the US in her 20s. She writes stories about her life and those of people she knows. Her goal is to enrich Asian cultural heritage and history to enhance cultural understanding and acceptance among all people.

**Andrea Abbott** has had a variety of careers including prison librarianship and ministry. She currently volunteers in the Spiritual Care Department at Upstate Hospital.

# Dear Reader

If you enjoyed this book, please leave a review to help other readers decide if this is a book they will enjoy.

If you would like to read more of Apple's literary journey, including news, updates, freebies, media coverage, etc., please sign up for her free newsletters at https://appleanbooks.substack.com/ or with the following QR code.

*Apple An's Book Bytes*
*(AABB) Newsletters*

**Thank you!**

# Daughter of Blue City

A Novel of Coming-of-Age Through Revolutionary China
© 2025

In the turmoil of China's Cultural Revolution, young Lianlian's life is shattered by family violence, public shame, and crushing poverty. Raised by a resilient but scarred mother, shadowed by an abusive father, and anchored by a little sister, Lianlian learns to survive a life with an impossible future. When the political climate shifts, she discovers that her mind is her only weapon and education is her only hope. Fueled by fierce determination and the quiet support of her mother, Lianlian battles for a spot at a top university, seeing it as her one true path to a life she can call her own.

If you like books about Chinese culture by **Amy Tan, Lisa See**, and **Pearl S. Buck**, and books about coming-of-age such as *A Tree Grows in Brooklyn* by **Betty Smith**, you will like this book!

*"A deeply moving coming-of-age novel."* – **Derrick Meade**

*"Impossible to put down."* – *TQ Pub*

*"What touched me most was how her mother and sister gave her quiet strength."* – **Sammy Moon**

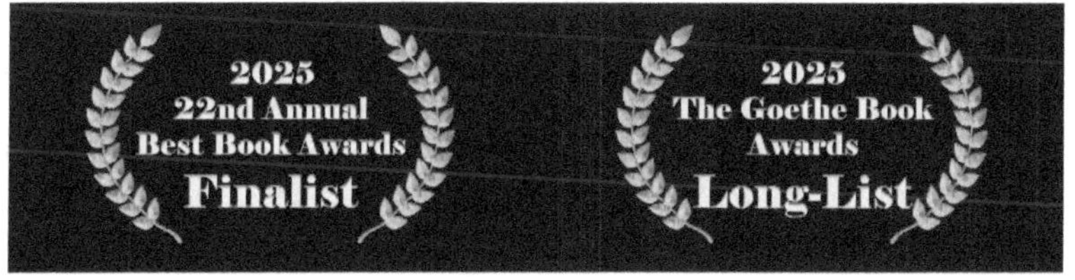

# Mother of Red Mountains

A Novel of a Woman's Journey Through Revolutionary China
© 2024

An ambitious civil engineer desperately wants to protect her baby girls in the shadow of China's tumultuous mid-20th century. Despite tragedies in her childhood, Jun crafts a stable life by changing her name twice to fit in a male-dominated and politically charged society. Ambitious and high-achieving in her career, she seeks help from her in-laws to care for the girls. But the in-laws' capitalist class makes them all prime targets for the Red Guards at the onset of the Cultural Revolution in 1966. Jun worries about the well-being of her toddler girls, as they constantly witness their grandparents, and their own safety, being violated. Will Jun triumph over the grave danger she encounters and successfully protect and maintain a stable life for herself and her babies?

*"Historical fiction/drama at its finest."* - **Pikasho Deka**

*"Lucid storytelling."* - **Carmen Tenorio**

*"I was transferred into this character and went through this journey with her."* - **Harley Grace**

*"The emotions feel universal and timeless."* - **Hopper**

# Las Crosses

An Unwavering Journey to a New Life in America © 2023

Fleeing the aftermath of the Tiananmen Square crackdown in 1989 and fueled by a burning desire for a better life, Apple embarks on a daring journey to pursue her doctoral education in America. With no backup plan, Apple must make this journey work. But she has no idea that her starting place, Las Cruces, NM, is a quiet desert town - a far cry from the bustling metropolis she envisioned. Anxious, ignorant, and homesick, Apple faces challenges she never had before. But she is determined to be open-minded. Excited and curious, will she simply survive the fish-out-of-the-water situation many immigrants experience, or will she thrive in this unexpected American adventure?

*"A story of opportunity, bravery and self-invention that's as suspenseful and inspiring as it is quintessentially American." - **Jonathan Dee***

*"Powerfully depicts scenes, characters, and emotions with bits of comedy." - **Cate McGowen***

*"An enjoyable and essential read on cultural contrast from a historical era." - **Ginnah Howard***

*"An inspiring story of resilience, hope and joyful curiosity, even in the face of uncertainty and difficulty. Uplifting!" – **Diane Pienta***

# 28 Voices

Voices Heard Anthology Series, Vol. 1 © 2024

Every life is a story, and every story holds a lesson. Within these 28 intimate essays, a diverse group of authors invites you to witness their most defining moments. They recount the laughter and pain of childhood memories, the forks in the road that marked life-changing events, and the heart's journey through love and relationships. Feel the awe of childbirth and parenthood, the struggle of balancing family and professional ambition, and the courage it takes to adapt to a new culture. With raw honesty, they explore the quiet resilience found in coping with losses and the personal paths to spirituality. These 28 honest reflections on the journey of life is a testament to what we can all learn, and what we have to give.

*"Not gonna lie, some of these short stories really got to me. They're worth checking, just prepare yourself." - **Paul Hoon***

*"Some of these stories are difficult to get through due to the nature of the stories, but overall the anthology was a good read." - **Jake Jacob***

*"Written by ordinary people leading ordinary lives. How very relatable it is. I was enthralled by the talent that was gathered together to contribute to this book. I enjoyed it completely and I strongly recommend it." - **Shannon Brennan***

# All-in-One Dotted Journal Notebook

For a Busy, Productive & Mindful Life © 2023

Planners + Organizers + To-dos + Reminders + Trackers + Journals + Random Notes + Doodles + Nuggets of Goodness.

Do you have a busy life? Do you want to be productive? Do you want to have an efficient assistant to provide notes when you need it? Do you want to eliminate loose papers and memos? Do you want to have fewer notebooks or journals to deal with daily? Do you want to spend minimum time preparing your templates and more time to be productive and enjoy life? This All-in-One Dotted Journal Notebook might be just what you need.

Give this a try for one month. There is no need to waste money if it does not work for you. You can find examples to guide you to developing your own habits and uses.

*"Takes getting organized to a new level!"* - **Joseph Brennan**

*"I absolutely love this planner! If you're looking for an efficient planner, this is worth considering."* - **Angela Dorris**

*"I appreciate most about this notebook is the upfront guidance and examples. It inspired me to use the notebook in ways I never would have thought of."* - **Leon Edward**

*"I am pleased with the large number of flexible templates for my various needs."* - **Kateryna Hlushchenko**